Colin Simms

Colin Simms — selected bibliography

Trawling, privately printed, 1960.
Tearlach, privately printed, 1960.
Lives of British Lizards, Goose and Sons, Norwich, 1971.
Some Effects of Yorkshire Flooding (with J. Radley), Sessions Book Trust, York, 1971).
Pomes and Other Fruit, Headland, Sheffield. 1972.
Adders and Other Worms, Headland, Sheffield, 1972.
Working Seams, North York Poetry, York, 1972.
Bear Skull, North York Poetry, York, 1972. (Revised edition, 1974)
Birches and Other Striplings, Headland, Sheffield. 1973.
Modesty (Swaledale Summer), Headland, Sheffield. 1973.
Pine Marten, Seven Prints, Genera 14, York, 1973.
Tees Tributary, Genera, 1974. (Revised and enlarged edition, 2000).
Horcum and Other Gods, Headland, New Malden. 1975, 1976.
Jane in Spain, Genera, Newcastle-upon-Tyne, 1975.
Photosopsis for Basil Bunting, Headland, New Malden. 1975. 2nd ed, 1986.
Rushmore Inhabitation, Blue Cloud Quarterly, Marvin, SD, 1976.
No North Western Passage, Writers Forum, London, 1976.
Flat Earth, Aloes Books, London, 1976.
Parflèche. Galloping Dog Press, Swansea. 1976.
Otters: Ten Seals, Genera 16, Newcastle-upon-Tyne, 1976.
Voices, The Many Press, London, 1977.
Humility, Spanner, London, 1977.
On Osgodby Cliff, Curlew Press, Harrogate. 1977.
Windscale: Four Cantos, Genera Eds, Newcastle-upon-Tyne, 1978.
Midwinter Housewife, twisted wrist, Hebden Bridge, 1978.
Pentland, Shadowcat, Weardale, 1978.
Some Company (Tea at 40), Genera Eds, Newcastle-upon-Tyne, 1979.
Hunting Bunting, Luksha, New York & San Francisco, 1979.
The Artist-Naturalist in Britain (Maxiprint, York, for the York Festival, 1980).
Spirits, Shadowcat, Weardale, 1980.
Movement, Pig Press, Durham, 1980.
Time over Tyne: Poems, The Many Press, London, 1980.
A Celebration of the Stones in a Watercourse, Galloping Dog Press, Newcastle, 1981.
A Second Book of / Look at Birds, Genera Editions, New York, 1981. (2nd, 1989).
Ingenuity (Wensleydale Winter), Shadowcat, Weardale, 1979.
Cuddie Cantos, Bellingham, 1986/7. 2nd edtn 2000.
Eyes Own Ideas, Pig Press, Durham, 1987.
Luigi Pirandello: Navigator, Shadowcat, Weardale, 1988.
Hunderthwaite, privately printed, 1990.
In Afghanistan: Poems 1986-1994, Writers Forum, 1994. (2nd enlarged edition, 2001.)
Poems to Basil Bunting, Writers Forum, London, 1994. (2nd enlarged edition, 2001.)
Shots at Otters, RWC, Reading, 1994.
Goshawk Lives, Form Books, London, 1995.
Bewcastle & Other Poems for Basil Bunting, Vertiz, USA, 1996.
Pine Marten: Fourteen Marks, Genera, 2003.

OTTERS and MARTENS

Colin Simms

Shearsman Books
2004

First published in the United Kingdom in 2004 by
Shearsman Books,
58 Velwell Road
Exeter EX4 4LD.

http://www.shearsman.com/

ISBN 0-907562-50-7

Acknowledgements:

The paragraph by Basil Bunting on page 9, and the excerpt from a letter by Basil
Bunting on the back cover, are reprinted here with kind permission of The Estate of
Basil Bunting. Copyright © 2004, The Estate of Basil Bunting.

Pages 13-31 of this book previously appeared in the collection *Shots at Otters* (RWC,
Reading, 1994), although three poems appear here in revised versions. Some of the
other poems collected in this book previously appeared in the following books, exhibits
and journals: *Derwent Frieze* (York Curriculum Development Centre, 1974), *The
New British Poetry* (Paladin, 1988), *Bewcastle and other poems for Basil Bunting*
(Vertiz, 1996); *Bear Skull* (Headland, 1972); *The David Jones Journal, Fire, Form
Books, Headland, Iron, The Northumbrian, Poetry Review, Weardale Gazette,
Working Seams.*

One poem was first 'published' on the wall of the *Criterion* pub in Hexham. Others
were broadcast on radio stations KRAB and KTCY in the USA.

The following have been critical and helpful over the years: Holarctic colleagues; Miss
M.M. Hartley was responsible for fair-copying recent versions of much of the text;
Miss J. Ufford and Mrs L.A. Simms are amongst the many who should also be thanked
for much support, and many others are mentioned in the text.

CONTENTS

OTTERS

Shots at Otters
Watter had vitalled	13
Aggregate melt-water remembered in him...	14
Now that the rivers are bringing down some loam	15
Poaching up North Tyne without a leistor	16
lochside silverschistsand disturbed-to-black-below distributed	17
follow the otter	18
Green-bottle-blocks kelp-racks raise lumpily rubbing-slumping back	19
As you move across the room lines of a fault in the windowglass run	20
tell me if you know where the heart of man goes	21
Rank-tidestrandside neap	22
dibble out a mandible tight in stalactite	23
Intak-downhill-sodcastmending old man...	24
the place had quiet in it	25
Decoy backswamp willowgarth jetty	26
itch all	27
Otter dead on the fell	28
thumping gavel	29
Waterbailiff, it was	30
Stiff enough	31
Watters abate at tides' hesitate	32
Sea Watch, S.W. Eire 1961	33
Outwits sight of the hound who doesn't know his scent	34
Sea Otters, Washington Coast 1973, 1981	35
Its whistle	36
sleeping off a good heavy feed	37
North Duffield and Bubwith	38
Otter Midden	39
Working the Otter	40
– Otter (is Not)	41
the calls they make are thin	42
walking waterline	43
molecatcher the otter has its fishing-seasons	44
Sea Otter	45
Solway Otter Sideways	46
By the Seph	47

(Westmorland, 1978)   48
Otter and Fisher   49
Otters in the Kirk Field Burn   50
Even if they don't hear   52
Snow shrank back to black lines alang banks and dykes   53
Squamish   54
Otter in Floods   55
Dog otter of Corsenside whose burns   56
Meeting a riverine marten whilst waiting for otter   57
The dog otter with a damaged paddle   59
alders bend over burns where their otters turn   60
Otterscat / at Derwent floods 1999   61
I thank you, Villon, for much   62
Lyvvenit; otter rived (it)   63
Young otter's shrill call   64
Vik on Alaskan coast owns   65
Nov. 16, 1997   66
Scargill Otter   67
Otters swim often near the surface, little dips under   68
Corpses, living   69
the moon not yet up, but the comet is   70
follow the otter   my fellow   71
Dytiscid Beetles in Redesdale   72
At the Farmer's Arms (Muker)   73
Otter, Redewetter   74
Otters at the Crossgill Gorge   75
bridge over river   76
the place had quiet when in it   77
(We'd been on the Tyne mouth for fish)   78
for Roy Laidlaw, Jed Forest   79
Otter, for Richard Hugo   80

MARTENS

Three Years in Glen Garry	85
nodding is trotting-on in bees, humblin	86
breath-taking you lose him	87
Marten-Smitt Spots	88
Marten gait Schubert's 5th Symphony / The Running of the Fox	89
Chestnut('s hissing)	90
Starling, when it is almost over,	91
falling-over notes and	92
Great Lakes Woods	93
A way of martens through trees	94
(Northern Ontario Jan 1976)	96
One gin trap less	97
The Weasel of Great Smeaton	98
We live in all around us, Joy	99
Kits at Midden:	100
(Marten and lizard / moved on / after more sheep to come)	101
The soil no longer soil	102
off / sun soft as ease	103
7 May 1987	104
Aeolian	105
He *came on a second, and, after, the fox;*	106
Cisa Appenina between Milan and Pisa	107
American Marten in Northumberland	108
Long-tailed weasel	109
(from some Welsh fieldwork)...	110
Starting the Night-Shift	111
Isn't Listening	112
(Male martens have 'rests'....	113
in the broken lands of the Ketilness	114
Running wick, leaping, loping, "sent"	115
"Lucky you got that skin; good news!"	116
Mart out of the trees beneath the thistles	117
March nightsweat, wondering where winter went	118
Marten, anchored into tree	119
Finned around pale bole old cottonwood	120
Castoring swivels big at ends of legs	121
scuffle at the double, Little Jack Russell	122
The day proved almost same gloom	123
Marten are in the ruined biggin	124
Only showing as dark wing-brushes	125

Marten at Rydal   126
Walking and working the many miles all weathers   127
Burren, Martens 1   128
Burren, Martens 2   129
(Mart – with Beryl   130
(S. Grillo, Brenda Richardson)   131
Antelope Marten Antelope Flats (Wyo '97)   132
March 20; Cuddy's Day   133
Feb 1st 1998   134
Least-weasels not so soft in tones   135
Marten lit / middle of wet   136
Marten deceives his pursuer (me...)   138
Nov. 3   139
Nov. 14 1997 / Eden   140
Marten and Otter   141
Mart, between squirrel-tail, puma-tail   142
It was, I suggested   143
Marten rising   144
Marten Hunting   145
A day I didn't see marten   146
Batting at Hawnby   147
(He wanted to give his Army compass   148
Marten, North Riding Coast   149
(Sister)   Jean, Rockies 1973   150
(from Tea at 40)   151
Vigil Trapline   152
Nov. 8th 1970 (Scarth Wood)   153
American Marten, Replacing the Pine Marten in England   154
At White Craig Picnic Site, evening June 4, 1997   155
Marten and Wild Cat   156
(Carcajou) Marten poems   157
brushing window his hail   158
weak as the sound is, it's   159
Lines   160
Turdus torquatus   162
Marten in juniper thickets   163

OTTERS

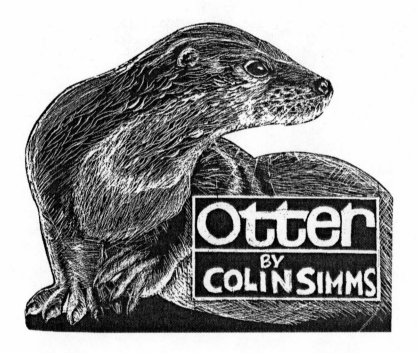

Otter
BY
COLIN SIMMS

"It is a few minutes only since we were looking at fresh otter seal almost at our doorsteps, and the thrill has not diminished since other occasions down this Tyne at Scotswood, up the Coquet and Allens and all manner of Northern waters up to seventy years ago. Colin Simms has a scientific treatise on otters being cautiously put together, but I hope this collection of his observational poems, pieces which first brought his work to my attention, will stand as a celebration of otters and their freedom, for the discerning. Long may the wild wanderer, and the unashamed poet, be at liberty to choose the way and where of living even to-day."

Basil Bunting, Greystead 1983

Watter had vitalled
that wettens now
blood leif to leave
treasured and swelled
as taints in current
air over the river
so they grow green-ness
by the same stones marked
blood leased by leeches
long passion decides
length and strength

nourished, gi'en blood
wattles and muddied
of its pressure
smells …. unhurried
spraints meshed and measured
arrested   even stones
as his muzzle will, heedless
          where the flood reached the moon
stone-loaches the otter ett
where floodwater subsides
                and tides

Otter Dead in Water (Drowned by 'keeper) 1984

Aggregate melt-water remembered in him his territory this dog-otter
Scarlutra, Scargill Beck otter   bigger, as hill fox is bigger
the same as only a few thousand years back to impermanent ice
may it be.   Many a bitter winter since.   This one skates ice like Skarp-Hedin
this otter - makes - water   of grass
on land elements blend but in water this one braids and beads, surfs and lines
Swale to Tees   defines and defies   rain on the wind
nothing to litter eleven canoes in a wild weekend of one storm
the fastest rise in England after a storm these rivers his utter delight
repose displaced from the river's loads to avoid   learns ditches
adapts raffishly   leaf-beat,   bits of stick,   stranded fishes
ground slick froth   white-grime of flood-debris
makes the water work for him   some fish leap for him, all-found
leaves gleam sticking to everything, all around.

Bowes, 1970

Now that the rivers are bringing down some loam
of husbandman's love off these enlarged winter fields
not merely silt, which would quicken water meadows,
they've cleared the willows to speed the water's flow.
Ings, otters' homes, all else of alder-carr goes
a balance of centuries to the balance-sheet yields.

Floods will increase, and still they gripp
uplands, deep-plough for the new forests, let rip
earth-movers to straighten courses in places
they curse as stagnant, and drain out the bogs
had held the rain in, sphagnum, let it go slowly.
Nature reasserts with storms and man's span
is merely money washed out with dead moles and voles
more for the crows. Lost less slowly; frogs and otters' graces.

Vale of York floods 1968   *for C.M.R. and M.E.B.*

Poaching up North Tyne without a leistor
and in thin moonlight right-minded Oliver
heard a splashing coming, glinting lit-silver.
Oliver Davidson swung once, and gaffed an otter!
A heavy and long and fit and fussy dog-otter;
his follow-through such that the ruddery monster
landed up on the mossy bank above our Oliver –
the more surprised, whether exulting man or insulted otter
we'll never know! But Oliver toppled over into the water
laughing after the otter cantered away, with a chunter.
Laughed at bruises big as cobbles coming later, did Oliver
but got his fish in that pool, anyway, evening after;
"got a verra bad chest for weeks, thought'd have it forever"
You can hear such gathering-burns laughing their way to the river

from Oliver in Tarset 1979

lochside silverschistsand disturbed-to-black-below distributed
pattern-padded pewter-grade velvet-hollows grains added otter pattern
wind off water levelling sibilant bevelling gritscreen bankscree
whistle   reminding you of   distant wigeon whee-oo
lifting, see prints between bents-tail-race-slice-silt sift sting
still tracks slow upslope shorten portage not forage but for ages
we newcomers can begin to see pattern   even from this little elevation
braids loosen elements-stream raise islands   bruised-
petal-heartsease-violet trail wakes prospect of please not violence
increasing-in-confidence   bolder heavier just before lost in boulders

     when we were least aware the stiff log dogging windshore
sure-of-his-lie breaks cover sure-of-his-line leans lie of the land over
from under could not-have-hidden-him right-under-feet wonder
instead left-right losing-using his whole enters not-in-the-line-of-his-head
twisting quick long into the river's plaited-in on-itself longitudinal as time
otters were here before
might be   but rivers were like that
if there is still any life in them

Loch Maree 1970

follow the otter   my fellow
river my side-brother   running where put
(and no other)   and in own mind   find
the land running through is rich re-instating
relating each meaning to each
each belonging to each, the bushes bending over
the river no more to be said to belong to any one
than anyone of its waterdrops in the circle, the cycle
through sea and sky than any one of its many flies
may-flies living mere hours with man the air shared
above the river surface mingling wind and water
quiet turning of willow leaves on its is
smile on the face of the fisherman's young daughter
caught in and made by the reflection, as of the leaves
have to be perceived together, alternative routes to the otter
are the roots of the otter and all other otters in their turn
take turn here, the dragonfly, even the sulky fish
it is for them only the beginning of their spontaneity

The River Derwent, Yorkshire, 1975

Green-bottle-blocks kelp-racks raise lumpily rubbing-slumping back
deeper than slurping the-word-for-it-waiting sit in the rockslit waisting
lenses swim perspective, help stack: cut-lawn; algae back-stooked raked
enlargement grates, grit-to-pebbles-to-boulders
cliffs round-off sky the same full tide overhead smooth grey west out-over
hull-low undulate us that; was-that-dog-seal head-up down-back-bob
nothing dents noting slabgrab at flab foam cream-off serpulid graffiti
gravestones denying any present even as same head rears reluctant ears nearer
defining otter: a feeling: not even a shape: agape; without form offer
firm man in the cleft of the sky closed anemones torn fronds away
midwinter turned the deep dive its pool debris brings the otter up again
all rudder and silver submarine steel nose tightlipped at the full quiver
little disturbed stones whisker to scale again the otter no matter of monster
but smaller than sea seal kelp, boulder wave braver keener denser than wind
                                                                    that way.

near Peel, Isle of Man 1964

As you move across the room lines of a fault in the windowglass run
the two otters mist tipped together motes on pages
together-gathered guard-hairs grazed
short frost-lipped furred-grass run
must not touch the hush-hard through it seems it is not reel
anglers commute away complete with bags and boxes mutter a little steam
feel hear the warning like a slapping on water for otter soul
we are in a martial thing poles-pikes-advance
hair-up-at-back-of-neck dog-soldiers
tails up even at rear of ruck
leader strikes scent
everyone rises to something eskimo taut about every hunt hurt at heart
nothing like
fast toward black centre from grey sides somewhere past to the cave hides
                                                              from the sun

Northern Counties (Tees) hunt, 1960

tell me if you know where the heart of man goes
with no shallows to play in after he's stopped lunging for tiddlers and tadpoles
with no clay banks to slide down, for to chute the right way when he grows
committed to gun and cunt struggling upstream dislodging setstones as he slows
not after otter but not content with a blank day
shoots the one he watches playing on the way where I was watching on the other side
like at the asylum-landing at Rawcliffe, Harrison riverman studied their muddy ride
cubs and parents year after year York folk never harmed them until the turn of tide
after the war brought more steel back home
and you don't hear them bark or whistle near the busy boatyards any more
or they go linked-arm by the willows or lifting skirts to the flood-mud shore
and the island hover even the 'touched-in-the-head' kept-in-the-head where he saw
otters above ground in daylight, otters chasing moorhens,
so that boys only had been initiated to it when they were sure.

Cascades Oregon hunt 1973

Rank-tidestrandside neap
smooth furred skin coming away from sealscorpse stained by slurry
ships-oil-can and boxwood
piles of fish-with-the-best-bite-out rot, oiled guillemot
with difficulty recognised with salt slant eyes memorised
the old dog-otter one-foot-short reduced to a scold natter of bones and scavenge
with dog-fox one night and the dog the next, near sized
still had open eyes from the drifters' revenge
on the North Sea, the dump of damned sprats in heaps, neeps too many for market
moon threat over them
sun not needed
godwits receded after wet horizons reducing sluicing polluting slicing diffuse
place defused of one power cracked for oil   lit up chemical underwear
detergents deproof otter underfoot.

Seal Sands, Teesmouth 1965, 1976

dibble out a mandible tight   in   stalactite
badger it loose carefully   prized or might-be-otter
compare   osteologically   to be fair
the weasel-family   share   some structure

concerned to discover what-comes-up-from-a-place
hard impressions to put flesh on   lines-to-a-face

but we don't know individual-behaviour-same-stricture
what river-otters were *doing*
to be interred in high-ridge caves   even in human burial-cysts
                an accidental   en-fracture
          what when these high-dry hills were not
high dry hills but
so "what does it tell you   what is it worth"
decent-clearing-events of small patch of an old earth.

bonecave, North Pennines 1969

Intak-downhill-sodcastmending old man, unloads breath slow hands cold
clouds sharpen sun, race fells run eyes (Arkle makes Swale sparkle)
up from alders   beck, check what made look
in gloom under elders-alive-hung like a beacon beckons for a second
alive the uncertain water above while the sun for a hover
the stem gold the fling silver-and-gold the new alder-leaves old-gold
watter whitefroth around teeth with effort the otter gleans the eel
from those stones the fish is wet fur under-hand-over the shower of light
shift-of-dragonfly pull-on-cord other times   the bell rung in-the-head
tussleing to see tousled to gain the thing beyond stones is scales
sun in the air descant-to-the-waters   variations and unhung
descends current for a better grip   swinging side to side the ends
already fraying the slime sticking dry stones in dying braying unsteady
crunching coarse gravel grumbling and whickering whiskers slip.

Swaledale 1955

the place had quiet in it
only passing on the road was noise processionary
so mist was encouraged distance discouraged
same process of time not engaged
so it was no out-of-the-ordinary thing
for the otters to be breeding here again
its flatness gained no out-of-the ordinary thing
between Pennine and Hambleton hills spraint-stains
it was steady May-time — early, even that not necessary:
it was the fill of the place between vague ranges
that weren't utter lines of space but own signs rearranged
receding, an approach acceding to reproach or effacing its own space
head-landed by drains to the field-corner pond when the pains came
she-otter come rudder from muddy-anglers'-landings
straining inland the barley-beards made eyes water to shudder
the heavy time of summer-not-yet but stillness
so blossomed as under snow but yellow king cups focal of this plain
locking marsh sockets locating watercourses mocking lanes
mist making parallax shift hiding any season some of the time
low to the ground gravid stutter slow so distributed sound
there might have been otter or badger or some other shudder
you wouldn't have believed the place could have stood
the rub romp cubs drubbed-ramp
or its air would stir between hairystem shrubs
their odour of stubends don't soil air or earth or water

Vale of York 1968

Decoy backswamp willowgarth jetty
duckweed decked dimple spread stippled to ripples
when a prime carnivore turns aside to reach elderberries
this un's   leadin   fur freedom
feel mental-real wriggling fundamental eel of a mammal

Underbank overhang alligator al'tigither
up the spout eel pout zander
scrattin tayties at Lillin Park tekkin boddincowls Julien Park
half a crown a day all the hours godsends   the otter for granted
es allus'theer
melting for head to bob grass is watterwessel   passin Sweet Fog Holcus
like the sun draws the damp out of the medders to mek fog
hairs out of algae jelly will mek't'frog

paralysed belief   otter   frozen in grief.

Yorkshire Lower Derwent and Eastern England 1972

itch all
each every sort of branch on its own rhythm;
switches across vision   twitches across eyes blindingly
deceivingly: deceitfully: increasingly every branch a breeze
all sorts of contrary winds:- spins dreams in the afternoon
Marshstitchwort as soft as Lady's Bedstraw   perhaps
the same swing is in the otters lolloping
moving - under   he is hunting known fetches
felicitously   never forgetting to look under each log
turn over each slape stone   he is hunting
generations   the gutters each utterly tested
tenacity   in transit
inch after inch
reach after reach

Norway

Otter dead on the fell   crunched rose-quartz skull
corbies already raking away   mandible, braincase with grey
dripping streamers of it   fellow flyingbent...yellow

no use asking the pipits

Pads cold, belly warm of decay   grin at crushed chin
caught in the open or brought there mutilated   dew on pelt
miles from the nearest place I'd ever found spraits   flat as felt
the whole scotching empty and quiet yet full and watching   brittle

months later the farmer:
the shepherd: the waller:
the huntsman: asked; no shepherds' route, and no walkers' "ever"
"hunting otters was finished"
"otters nae harm".

Years later a whole family taken away
probably for "sport", as badger-baiting
from a holt not far away
"who'd want the cubs
and what for".

thumping gavel
Otterburn Ranges explosions beyond
'Otterburn' may not refer to otters at all:
better stay with stumbling literacy than clever unravel
if it severs youth's unabashed travel and your brother's
staying hours and midges for one shrill whistle.
Rede's moontreading, already a pressing
redds gravel falls syllabic for trout or salmon
puttering starting-up as there, the loose papers
even the stone-loach! Happy to show watter-ranny.
Low as river is, it carries far   unravel   a fear, rapid
otter utters   starting-up   puttering two-stroke
whicker and chatter pattering papercrisp leaf-furl
inches a fear   onto portage   hesitates
men- and mink-scents near, anglers' pitches warp
windloosed leaves but soft
onto dewgrass by design
wept into my face

'Redewetter', for Anita 1988

Waterbailiff, it was   told me about it
midwinter Mirk Esk   asking some renewal
silver line thread fine   telling his beads
treadle but rhythm   rattle of miresnipe
(no more by hand   language   even *this* land)

nor by smell
months after the midwinter hunt
with the thaw I worked beck and burn, stell and eals

furtive old soaked rolled-rag cliprug love-atrophied
all-falling envelope of stench held it together
knocking-soft against my knees in the spate
I bent in unhooking spent fish
as the fur came-away   bloat-white green-liquid
tumbled, contusions tough skin still showed
glowed bacterial – head and tail gone to trophies

stones fine-comb that clean burn
silvertress water-goddess
stress on line-endings.

Cleveland to Border
Esks

Stiff enough
wind to slough
a stubborn rise off the riffles
hardly spray, much
last little frass up off stubble

reach after reach of this river
lifts its drift to more-than-mist
Scot's mist scotched by its vigour
face stinging sifting scour
has watervoles stooked, chattering
little agitated castanets six
to ten to the bar, crescendo alarm
or challenge, shivers with shimmer
before the otter shod a sliver
only of self above surface
moves in it smooth as if he knows
deceit of it mirage as moonbow's
above and lighting up the show

Watters abate at tides' hesitate
as at a foss moment of spate-lessens/losses
(the hollows of the ripples down a sike/lonnen)
shortened to such a drag or stop
vowel overtops the beat; a fall is on the cusp/at the lip
but some momentum carries us over/off
Otter being carried down the flood
is at danger at the bridges, is tobogganing
all elbows and rudder, may not see the danger.
No - his head is up through the rapids' shudder
spreads himself, braking between the boulders
of glass. Time crops off heart of the watcher
lamely at the bridge otter climbs out of the water
to portage, shaken at amazement of watterdrops

Swaledale 1956/68

Sea Watch, S.W. Eire 1961

froth, minds increase with the tide and to match
something required of us; form and froth mesmeric
walked the strandline westward as far as the Point
rocks and pools and wind buffets tossed off cliffs
gannet diving far out, just arriving other gannets
further out, our eyes accustomised finding stars,
Baily's-beads and your own blood at the speargrass scratch
barely accountable cut if the bed accosted us
line of blood just rising something swelling out far

ebb tide's further back-ring something within us hatched
where his footprints had come over ours at a tangent
since we had arrived, had so much time passed, even?
And whose bobbing in the sea where we had watched,
turned aside to make love, as a response to him
his weaving wave kelp slenderer than on land.
Whose grace we had not slandered by suddenness
as we had before; but by the lady's bedstraw
prepared, and bruised ragged robin, and avens

for J.D.S.

Outwits sight of the hound who doesn't know his scent
not the dyke-back where the fox has marked and narks
      by using dead-ground
      whipper-in precisely as long
hounds and
as is needed

fired-up for destruction   otter-shooter

faces up to the otter but blunt between his boots and so sudden from nowhere he shudders
and misses
whether any such eel could go as quick
then wonders

remembers a sea-trout under a tree-root
this is a part of the power of otter.

laughs at the naturalist and has brokken
and sucked those eggs, even the eggs
Before the breakfast-maker was woken
the necks of this theory — chicken in Middleton
he had overlooked
eggs laid with strychnine for foxes

otter-hunters' "singlesticks" shingle squeaks
      rasps

as otter at Winch Bridge squelches and jarps whinclitter
reminding me of such names as East Winch
(coarse East-Anglian)Heacham   Clenchwarton
      (otter after whelks)

N. Counties' hunt

Sea Otters, Washington Coast (Olympic Peninsula 1973, 1981)

       longshore   rockrib groin

rorquals rib runs royal squib seastack stub stumps of de-inhumed hill cores;

      play is the tide's lick at the smooth rocks ruck it hydraulics suck it

raft-cork, a hummock a tussock proud of kelp mats at bottlegreen surface oil

ostler caresses horseflanks, testy butler carrying tray some 80' and more, jostling drift

stripped spears distal timber my fears in the water, tumbling slowly revolving according

to tide and current a matchstick dance at a distance, whole horizontal mazes of them

plumbs to a floor only the sea otter makes sense of, walks safe on meniscus

catlike for all it is heavy with water the tail comes up, graceful and playful

perfect harmonic curving complexity   belying its heaviness as Oliver Hardy's his

its wave going on a little in the air beyond its tip, the air over the kelp, after the actual

motion in the animal has finished; but of course the animal is hardly ever at rest;

like the river otter in playfulness, in making the water one with it, doing things for it

water and air, as a dolphin's water might be, water as rarefied air a stir

Its whistle

water such that
under the horizon to horizon flow

so that the weir at Chollerford   here
is hidden, drowned under a long slant of break of slope lost
like the Roman bridgepoint a little downstream

they who pursued Jock of the Side
stopped beside this water   big but not as big as this
didn't dare go through

river takes the otter away with it
melting some innocent we averr

Its whistle panpiping bellows below
its following fellows
                        in the silence
                        insulance
                pumping where the rocks curve over
crowd   river passage, former channels, spate-concaves
walls is what they tender under
walk   already   bubbles
                then   surface again
as the Little People   alongside Athabascan Algonquin Iroquoian

*Charles Laughton's direction of the flight of the children
down under in 'The Night of the Hunter' (1955)*

sleeping off a good heavy feed

for a day or more after it

otter

their eyes glow round marbles of glass in the moonlight
as much as in torch light

their squealing, light but
penetrating whistles   the noise of a bird rather than a
mammal – though some other mustelids can make very similar calls –
especially the young

The whistles of kingfishers can be
similar – their challenges and excited chicks as the parents pass
Sometimes the otter's call as long drawn out
as a boy can prolong wet finger squeal on glass

North Duffield and Bubwith

                                frogspawn and footprints made by an otter
                  for   my daughter a mile upstream of the bridge
              a   portage to yield   on the balance-account
        the river demands this field   by proxy   laid-down amount
     feathers   of moulting mallard and shoveler softly stun the mud
    the otter had stopped to snuff ridge-back down-snout up-blood
apex   we cut at   the base of she will not forget this   river
    brought to her feet so deep a trickle   I thought she'd weep
    until the heron steady asleep or fishing reflection a shiver

Otter Midden

N.E. coast

like some of the tideline stones
we knew them crush them on with heavy blows
the tones of *Lutraria lutraria*
the otter shell, as he saw so well
and showed me the brown/grey tones
of the head and nape*   upper breast
and the off white yellow of the bib below
the textures of that shell
                no surprise to find the fragments
in my fingers from the otter's feeding bench salty
and in the scats, more comminutely

*which are all the otter often shows, you know
as the wildfowler, angler   glow
            those who see them in the water
reasonably easy either to open (hinge is not midway along the shells 'back')
or to crack – we washed the 'cross cut'   shell sherds also
broken on these middens
           and, of course, plenty of mussels

for J. U. and L. U.

Working the Otter

further out over the bigger river
than angler can cast or poacher leistor
or net; a place to work the otter is set
between two men, one either bank, in moonlight
or simmerdim, one will catch the otter and one the bailee!
weighted keel, like the otter's rudder   ye kna
will bring him back to the bank in any river

my otter derived from a toy destroyer
cut from solid   by Uncle Bill long since lost superstructures
(stuck on with glue water and rough usage loosened
we drilled her side as for oars and stuck dowels in rows
each to carry its line and beetle-baited hook
different lengths – some just pricked fish
(caught a crab) some caught fish the real otter took!

- Otter (Is Not)

wethead   weight   but bulk
silkstrokes   lodestone   but arrow
flagstones fast paddle linking puddles with lithe light
airthins   cannot be held   I'm thinking   sackskins
utterly wet your body slumps   but is not yet dead
the lead loaded   pole hasn't dealt put plumbed
death held off an instant a moment coming up now
for last breath reddening all the water here forever
no matter how often I come back I will come back
rub like you did against the bankstones, its terracettes
and the bark of alder and in the stiff thickets

"Dance to your shadows
There are tunes in the river,
otter pools in the river
hin, hin, haradalla"!
                    (Folk Song)

the calls they make are thin
neither a pipe nor a whistle
though they are often described as this –
one or the other, and they skim
or seem to skim from one
place on the river to another
above the river's own hiss
["Dance to thi daddy"]
though often like its seething
in the rain. And with lilt
such as the wind can give, filtered
in leaves and on the surface of it
the river is enhanced, the wind
in combination, altered
is, the trees' singing itself.
To act is to become *yourself*
and all join in on the dance
rapt, enhancing concentration
["thoo shall have a *fishy*"]

walking waterline   rising fast and heaving
burden-rolling   line-of-sight and bearing, leaving
tonight the Tyne   is running like the Snake *
jerking-off froth and leaping, backwards over
"hasting-doon"; white careers truncate
curves too boisterous ever to have been perfect
while the otter hesitates, waits on, erect.

Bluster of clouds and the full moon sudden, "lish",
backward-stabs the wind upward, which
is with-current sou'wester   whose freshet
is off the snowmelt birches-bent acknowledge
wave of the fell, alders lean-to gill-ledges
nearer the water than the otter, now he reaches
my scent; no alarm but flood's all-voices-up
including the boulders rumble of that undercarriage
the otter is avoiding – as he is the water-edges'
clarts and flood-debris bundled along. No fish
until he might find strandings on new beaches.

(* of Wyoming & Idaho)

1997, 2003

molecatcher   the otter has its fishing-seasons:
though dawdling full of easy-meat

unhobbled rivers rise with rain / and fall away
swell, and dwell and dwindle / again
noise increments with otter's boldness
all other noise decreases on the moment which is
pitches more than a reservoir / or a drain
living strain in molecules, time, ta'en
other lives gives not loss not gain
the living web is as this spraint's painstrain. *
Young otters already know to fish these pools
when they rise, water and fish together
paint-stained masks muzzle no fools
clarts playthings in this soft weather
before the peat murk obscures the water
eels can't be fished under peat-taint spate.

*otter spraints often so broken, washed, crumbled and fallen
to resemble slivers of silt or lichen; encrustants even micaceous.

Sea Otter

racoon-fingering
wet cocoon
    animate bundles
    slow blue bubbles
  the whisker barbs whistle
    taps at my breathing
heaving seas' troubles

Kamchatka, 1981

Solway Otter Sideways

Tide to saltmarsh stutters   then sings
cormorant - stalwart attends to such things;
wings hung wide over gutters   folded-back
black and neck bent to watch on the wrack,
better on his guidepost than its flotsam-jarring ride.
We had been counting plover, dunlin, sanderling;
not a log there, drifting in on running tide
but a rag-bundle,   extended loose as that
ropeshank or oily waste ships' cotton, as black;
slack as his paws slung over and over, crabwise
rolled who had been wise to crabs, to crack and crunch
clawed off the bottom or caught-out in shallows
shadow-upward, of sand and silt, place lightly held.
Yet oddly dry, desiccated; only blood in the gut
when we opened it, the sodden fur still whole
as buffalo-robe whole. 'For all the blood-strew
in all the world springs in those cold kells'
of Border Country fells we returned him to.

By the Seph

I scythed to the Phalaris margin, the false-reed, silage-mocking reed;
the beckside at last, quiet the beck under the blade's long sizzle
last swathes this side of it but where otter cubs once mewed, those five Julys.
He who in his heart harbours under-worry a burning anguish
is naturalist and poet foddering, the old god's King Phalaris
tyrant; any poet sighs for imprisonment in such place as this Phalaris's
but hay has to be down to be brought to hairst, and otters not seen these five years.
Rather a hind understood by beast-kind than a poet misunderstood of man.
Scythe had reached as far and no further and the brunting music of the beck
took over.

(Westmorland, 1978)

>> a loping marten can sound
>> louder than a bear at night
>>> (and so can even a pheasant)

Otter on portage

Otter webs patter wet mud
(pattern: terrem terrem terrem)

free as a badger on tarmac
in the dark

> or a marten   puttering
among dry leaves (and so less clearly)
a line between trees
> like the marten vocabulary
> low escaping almost purring
repeated growl rowl woul uul

in fright   in flight
lope-length shortens for the Rydal Mount
> as if Wordsworth out of puff (never!)
gear changes because the way is steep
>> all poets have to be cross-country runners
>> Sid did, as Wordsworth did assent

>> our thoughts are louder
>> than our actions
>> because they disturb all
>> our other thoughts
>> and everyone else's if expressed

Otter and Fisher

Upright, for long tail fifth limb, pressed to the earth,
the fisher paused at its grooming in the rockfall
where I'd expected a marten that fall, its fissure
– they are not fishers though they don't scorn fish
I found from his kitchen-midden
(18 only hares, provision not for a family).
They are said by trappers to empty porcupines from beneath
and surely they are, with the carcajou, regular killers
           porcupine quills notwithstanding
         hedgehog spines to that otter
            we watched swinging it Rawcliffe/Clifton Ings
with Wilf Harrison, who'd noticed the stings
drew points of blood on his muzzle.

Balanced – triangle head super-marten proportions different –
very long tail, strong deep body and neck, and legs not so long;
between otter and badger in ground-cover wholeness,
marten and glutton somehow in bulk, and in boldness.
Repeated that osprey's show off your open window
widow Dorothy knowing ahead
        a few days before you died, well-wisher

for Ray Fisher, De Grey Rooms 1977

Otters in the Kirk Field Burn

This morning's wet and wearying miles before the dawn
the stumble in bramble and off stones in bog and gleg
with thanks to the moon, between squalls, in acknowledgment;
but tracked at respectful distance wandering dog-otter
across the fell down to his hover Kirkfield Burn
both of us inconvenienced, but hap not much by each other
having picked up a day's, or more than a day's, subsistence...

and he had done better than me, having been Visiting
where I had only been near one known denizen, dark his den
and he the poorest even of hill farming men (I didn't know that then)*
hours I froze in he played with bitch otter all dance-in-a-ring
all King-of-the-castle and splashing like children but still I jumped
for second-hand joy, (not matching the otters' greeting and tumbling
their whimpers and whickers, bickering sheer enthusiasm!)

• how he flung an eel in the air I had not seen him capture
• and she lept for it, and he knocked her over as she did so
• was she sibling or mate or potential mate, there was rapture
• noisy as two dogs, easy with each other as littermates, aglow
• in gloom and light alike, wind and shower, with exertions' haloes
• and sheens that wavered and rippled two 'barguests'
• or boggarts, as another hill farmer many years ago in the North Riding
• had shown me with pride, on just such a night, cloud signs racing
• before I lost the moon, and them, buoyant light struggled with stealth
• the rhythms something Mussorgsky's *Songs and Dances of Death*
• orchestrated here, phrases so near them, in steps and grunts becoming distant

Yes, but a day when most foxes are urban scoundrels and runts
and most otters tolerated and bound for tourist's theme-parks
will be as bad as any since bear begone and sparks
gave more early mornings to perfumed beds than hunts

(in which the chase is all, if well-matched, not the kill
but what we have now is too much convenience, overkill
even a *genuine* seduction is part denatured by The Pill

a few years later to burn down his house at the
injustice of having to pay an irrelevant 'poll tax' on it.

Even if they don't hear   people outside the anguish
the music is enough,   all the work, the waiting
Phalaris put his victims in the hollow brazen bull
burnt them to cinders slowly over, our frustrations
transformed their pain to song, reeds in the flaring nostrils!
for bronze bulls, or poets' some sort of liberation.
Next morning to gather hay by these the reedgrasses' stir
on drying wind black cattle over the hill baited still
fresh on Phalaris base blades an otter had sprainted there.

Snow shrank back to black lines alang banks and dykes,
crags' shelter and crest swales' shadders and sykes
dusting, just, in north facing spaced-out clitter
moment we sense a movement patter,   stutter
below the pitches we are here to climb
where beck's head rises in rockfall's springing line
Expecting fox or stoat from its slow stink
astounded ignorant big-bounding fummit
at otter forgot summit, felt intrusive...
Thirty years later the same sort of thing conclusive
then of our intrusion: otter killed by climbers
under the Callerhues crags.

"Snow is the extension of water into air and land
otters are waiting for; Menominee understand".

Squamish   'even seen otter fish
in the air'   with the bear air their water is
watchwelter   wheel turn on their tails, flailfroth
for their young   kicking kelts clear, as not of worth
their dying in, dirtying, the river
'River is Otter Way'
Progress their young to play with Spring Run
salmon trim yet full, clean-run.

For this the fresh one scarce a splash or a wash
humps with the river's short exhortations haughty taut poise
jumps complementary just poetry commentary wordsweet (from lumps)
otters one after the other romp air and water burn spray pelt
gleam – turn   loop run   and shake   sharpen their fur-points
out of water into water pricks and anoints.

Otter In Floods

for Elliott Ridley

(Garrigill)   Dec. 23, 1982

Loud stormclouds clot and scatter
downwind downstream dog-otter
follers the left bank, mair a potter
oftener than hunting the river
right foot dabbling in watter
patting at dents in it; dapples it
until onto stones, an' he straddles it

bubble-patterns reach me clustered
(as close as that), patterns of bubbles
delicate as when the dipper dabbles
he has been watching, has a stab at
right front paw as she passes under
on her business over the riverbed
– the spate has stayed trout; even crayfish

Yet he is not wet yet, never is (it)
and how far before me has he run it
and why? To surprise a water vole?
No riverside birds at this season
save the dipper (and the mighty heron).
Wrens and dunnocks, though, they come
and others attracted by the debris, scrum

Dog otter of Corsenside whose burns
boiled after thunderstorms kept himself warm
in the church of St. Cuthbert; after all
there was neither 'fighting at the ford'
nor wharrisname in his cell or stall
the hunter, and (land) owner John Thirlwall
who, like others, since, provided no priest.

He rolls over indulgent, paws in the air
and doesn't bother to ask anything at all
let alone why we were at love on that seat
when we could have been down in the perfumed fern
the sun warmed outside well north of the Wall:
his own parish/beat as great as Simonburn
and as many young bitches coming on to heat.

Joe and his father had seen in their youth
otter cubs play at the foot of the cross,
King of the Castle on fallen gravestones
while their old blind dog lolled, paws across
in a dream in the porch, denying the truth
'dogs don't need breakin to the otterhunt'.
This one had no appetite for bones .....

Meeting a riverine marten whilst waiting for otter, South Tynedale 1967

The 'isness', the specific nature, of martens is an elusive matter, and will vary with any observer, even one who tries to avoid what is 'said' already, what is 'expected' opinion. There are moments when the character of individual animals seem more accessible to us than at others, though it may be illusory to think so, and indeed to think that what we see can be interpreted satisfactorily in accord with any presumption or supposition. There are moments we are granted which are, however, whatever their 'significance', utterly unexpected and charming...

The marten halts short of where the otter had, some weeks before, when he also got my scent; a function of the breeze moving riverside trees a little, a breeze noticeable to me only along the river. Where the otter had perhaps been aware he would be silhouetted against open sky in the gap between the alders, the more so if he raised his foreparts on the tripod of his rear feet and rudder to get a good look over the grasses, this marten was perhaps more curious or less cautious. He rose on to his haunches first, which showed me only his ear-tips at that range and in that light, failing now, and then on what must have been his rear toes and perhaps also tail a moment; there were no tussocks there, often a marten will ascend part of a tree or bush, a wall or any other suitable height to have a look or try the scents. I was lucky and the slight wind at that moment didn't betray me. I was stock-still and not looking directly at the spot where waving grasses indicated the marten was shifting about a bit to get better vantage. Then there was a surprise; a low whinny more associated with the female marten and her cubs, and with her kits, in my experience. But this was a male animal, and he proved also to be alone, and, after that apparently querulous whinny, silent. Minutes followed 'dead' until I half-saw and half-heard him vigorously scratching and then shaking his fur – and I realised he was not merely gently grooming-out the water from his river-crossing but shaking it vigorously from his guard-hairs and combing it violently out of his fur including – I saw as I got nearer during this distraction – his tail; chasing it in tight circles and biting at it, soft-mouthed. I'd never seen this before. The picture remains in my mind to this day of the fun he was having; that the whinny was perhaps not of frustration or annoyance at the wet but more like the similar notes I've heard from otters, in anticipation, perhaps of the fun of the drying-frolic. I was not, I soon noticed, the only fascinated observer. A tawny owl was dropping almost quietly steadily down through the branches of a nearby large alder, eyes on the marten and not apparently noticing me and even to within a few feet both of the ground and of the marten. This reminded me of the 'fascination' small birds often show for playing, 'dancing' stoats and weasels; behaviour I've noted also for fisher, wolverine and least-weasel in North America, otter and kolinski in Eurasia.

Suddenly the marten whinnied again, and in a fussy, noisily abrupt takeoff the owl was gone, its draught almost dislodging my usual winter cap, and then the marten saw me, 'froze' a moment as I did, and then very slow-motionly and raised paw after paw as if trying cat-ice into what was become gloomy and misty night.

The dog otter with a damaged paddle
we traced over the years into three adjacent counties

Anita who Basil had insisted Ani*tra*
(dancing not needing to be other than her natural motion)

the same otter which (we) had met at the Lochmabenstone had nonetheless gone up
the Gelt and not the Eden; the South Tyne as if needing to ever get higher 'flying' ten
miles and more in a night the odd time we could be sure of it
        snows of Priorsdale wall-following, why this long way
                     had it been before into Teesdale?

1979
For B.B.

alders bend over burns where their otters turn
halt at their holts a day or a night, root-arches riven for caves
alders bend their burns, otter-routes in their turn
to the detail of pattern the burn might keep until floods' fetch
refresh it with deposit - but the rhythm still is in it
– in the otters' lives because of its dichotomy unity; learn
riffle and pool riffle and pool reach after reach and stretch

from head-over-heels at the sour-milk nick point,
(the watters little fosses), down to the clartiest wath,
are stumbled along a day after grey spraints and webbed prints
"he went this way", look; he's making airt for the wattersmeet
where she spread her cakes and beer, whisky and skirts
and we shared barely breathing where he had gone to ground
where Basil and our lady and I found rest as sweet

(modified 1997)

Otterscat
at Derwent floods 1999   (March 10)

river, reducing,   has a mind for spring and springing
sings out of the swelling soil of the ings, retreating (from winter)
from its flood levels this highest Derwent   the bits of the scat are
'oxidised' silver and black, tarry and stringy, not stodgy, dribbled rather than scattered
                                    as if Jackson Pollock and not the otter
or the freshet which came after separated and redistributed its elements
has been responsible   make its elements of its whole, to ferment
in my mind, firm-up   why not transported further?
I suppose the coil like a coit resisted shifting, even turning, adhesive
                                    surely the current would have
rolled these segments, segments, threads,   fish bones and scales

I thank you, Villon, for much:
but, if for nothing else then for this;
"winter is when wolves hang on the wind"

blow-balls arise, alone; which are not
of the turbulence above, their own stot
of the turbulence below bubbles that clot
and rise from waterspeed and the stones' plot.

The tallest man has a rusty leistor tied to his pole
its other end shod also of steel; wirebound against splitting
from heavy shocks – the whole strong enough to lever rocks,
..."both ends", said the Methodist minister "hard for harsh restriction"
..."as his life". Tight birth and expected death his own head and feet
has been, and was; and indeed I got to know this man
as having already been dead ever since sixty, having started
hard work by fourteen and his only relief killing fish and
killing their fishers 'sawbills' and herons and otters

his pole drove apart alder roots, gripping along the banks
disturbing water a reach downstream the otter there urges
into, to be seen less through its turbidity though she is tired
too tired to dive again readily, and floated like debris
she had already become before the great jaws' riving

both already dead then, yet this is the height of his career
at least, at last, already skinned out, measured by eye for the box
the trophy to be mounted in – not merely the mask for him
but the entire sullied pathetically small like the fox
he already had, that had taken less than his lifetime.

for E. Mottram

Lyvvenit; otter rived (it)
(even, this, the mid-'sixties)
rivetter steadying for the rhythmic hit

bracin hissel an dove intil dubh
head up and missing none of it

whear ligs; i' logwatter
until hoonds o' passed' tigither

One with the ripples
gone with the ripples

vibrations sit stipples on surface tension

mighty   shallow   catspaws
on the watters' surface seeming to oilsilk it
the squalls
(as if) hug swans' paddles   make them
softly levering for take-off
to raking – on that same solid surface to whight

easy to see the breath, and had, of Gods

1960's
Langavat

Young otter's shrill call
very like young meadow pipits'
the plaintive side of this pipe

When the moon was veiled
behind thin high cloud tonight
from time to time, there sailed
colours off the otter coat sheen
in its wetting; an aureole
parallel to the calling

June 17, 1980

Vik on Alaskan coast owns
where stiff the rollers loll
broadsides on the full humpies
sockeyes, steels, kettas, kings
wait with him for tide or wind's
freshet to ride in on to spawn
those he will not bother to kill
bites out shoulders and over-full
laconic spent as if already kelt

keep it clean of oil-industry
this North Slope to the Beaufort Sea
leave it alone for their liberty!

1981
1999

Nov. 16, 1997

so wet this night after moonlit ones
otter swam like fish in the longgrass meadow
its aftermath no beasts have cut these haughs
down for the yowes. Running in wet swallies
for the riversides alder and still-green sallies

hours on, with the sun, grass glows with her
flows with her run as the watter grows on weirs

Scargill Otter

Horizons range as you climb north from Deepdale Beck
aligned yet continuous (at your level, what?) above Deepdale (the) wreck
– line of limestone   like its reefs   sails reefed in/by
ragline of buildings.   Kine   farms and barns
their dykes and walls and swales and little rises   of old usage
nature outcrops   backsapping likes   itself; it repeats
or is in emphasis   (not denial)   it repeats itself
that is, : its nature and feature

Otters swim often near the surface, little dips under
break tension and ripple and slit its swell
that we want to see into. But we blunder
same clothes every day – they don't see very well
so why do we bother? It is part of our wonder
unthinking boys of all ages 'sense' about smell
water carries, and above the water a current
of such sure molecules as surely can tell
in their security we will be as content
with watching, taking our chance for the moment
not to live as otters live, the tides of light
and time, but to offer a trial of 'rime' *
Coquet defies the W. M. Davis grades
favoured rocks don't happen by chance
favourite hovers they used over our decades.
Though crossing their path is happenstance
'ignorance' inadequate confirms our trades:
if they can whistle, we can begin a dance
they in their dimension secret (perfect) have made
us once aware so more than a glance
their up and down of the head before
they whicker on greeting, as reptilian
as Darwin's lizards, Iranian monitor
Gila monster, the little ones in my wall
(comprehension we stubbornly struggle for)
the moment one accepts us individual;
otter, monument, "another concept to store"
shaking our heads in defeat and awe...

* in the sense of Duncan and Mottram

Corpses, living

Under, the waters of this lake
I watch for otters, are lapping
old birchsticks detach their lashed bark.
Corpses, package feral burial
unwrapping in the passage wake;
the whistle of the otter is a ripple.

Castle Howard National Wildfowl Count
10th Jan 1969

the moon not yet up, but the comet is
clear of the long limbs of rearing hills
its reflection blooms on these river pools
still in the cold, one after the other I gather
silver doubloons, ring brighter than the snow
old ivory dykebacks, a few flakes coming down
a harsh March dying hard, steel to the heels

leaning-rearing near the dog otter revealed
softer than riverstones, bolder even than cobbles
spate left to smoulder his telegraph-poles
spraint between creosote and molasses, hot pone
on the still air, so close clean dirt private messenger
spoke to silence between grunt and whimper
he's gone down-river between Redwing and Eals.

31st March 1996, Tynehead

follow the otter   my fellow
river my side-brother   running where put
(and no other)   and in own mind   find
the land running through is rich   re-instating
relating each meaning to each
each belonging to each, the bushes bending over
the river no more to be said to belong to any one
than anyone of its waterdrops in the circle, the cycle
through sea and sky   than any one of its many flies
may-flies living mere hours with man the air shared
above the river   surface mingling wind and water
quiet turning of willowleaves on its own axis
smile on the face of the fisher man's   young daughter
caught in and made by the reflection, as of the leaves
have to be perceived together, alternative routes to the otter
are the roots of the otter and all other otters in their turn
take turn here, the dragonfly, even the sulky fish
it is for them the beginning of their spontaneity

The Yorkshire Derwent, 1975

Dytiscid Beetles in Redesdale

Wouldn't have found one species
if the traffic to Redesdale Show
hadn't stunned its flight to the road
and inside my line; its metallic glow
and grooved striations having me slow
fold wings back under black shield wingcases.
Why should such a water-beetle *fly*
and where does a successful predator need to go
when this river's shallow pools are full of fry
and late tadpoles, all manner of larvae?
Thinking there's a restlessness in all predators
Basil and I come back, to await she-otter
peel out of the water, before it's quite dark
(they've even seen one in the Mill car-park)
and portage to where her cubs are hidden
'gladdening old eyes' secretly, more than eyes
mind, not to speak of until years later...
a second *Dytiscus* species, other shield-cases
discarded cubs' toys, perhaps, on her midden.
Behind the pub, weeks later, bidden Joe Graham
joins us. The haughs suddenly slough off
a ribbon of otters, reel off four quiverers!

1983: Dytiscus marginalis, Dytiscus dimidiatus.

At The Farmers' Arms (Muker)

Sheep talk, for they talk through these lads
an' they can rattle big sash windows
                              gert huge sandwiches
cabinet of old beer-bottles

a place where David and I picked up
a *Gavia immer* stormbound loon
which had fished the floods around Kisdon:
'Kisdon Island' in the great 18` century floods
took it on to Solway the next morning

we hadn't meant to sup at all at Mukerr
but what with oor Will an't' weather
ivvera hoor as ivver oor joint maistherrs
whenever weather, inner or, ivver, outer
                              an' we've had nae summer

on the road up here in't glum, an otter
Ernie and I fund ten yearrs aforre:
(half-remembered – it doesn't matter)
it was *that* quiet. As on Allen medders
Basil and I found another

Strawb beck

                    that way we knaa, hoo-ivver
"it'll nat be a lang winter, tha knaws"
creaters like dayleet otters kna better.

Otter, Redewetter

Explosions tumping gavel on Otterburn Ranges beyond
yes inclusions jewel never unravel
Rede's bed moontreads   gravel humping
redd syllabic sea-trout itches

Otter utters shrill   as low as this river is
rapid carries far
fisher men and mink hear, fear bewitches

No otter on to portage cotterpins anglers' pitches
torquelles starting-up two stroke puttering wingstroke
of rooks, of chainsaws corded   their roost where rattles
like papers putter patter   windloose leaves but soft onto dewgrasses
so close rank swell wrapt wept in your face:
others, a shortage of Good Fish.

Redewetter is Rede River, Northumberland.
For Bill Lawrence (1968)

Otters at the Crossgill Gorge

remind me of   at this wath, this watters plash
the otter hasster show hissel(f)
if til lig here, he mosst cum near
an' if its reet thee'll *hear*

as cum the season we'll harry a few
last yeear Ah pinned you in the Strother
after a fahve mahl run, an' yet it flew
at m'ankle, bit through, Ah still hev bother
Yer the lad, issn't ye noo
kemm awa(y) frae the Hunt dance
ter spy t'Skreek Hullets, yance
lang syne, bot it wer noatiss'ed, eh
at gawpin, thoo'll do weel eneugh
– whin ye're next; 'Sting 'mires chotch
leuk in the back pew an speer ti me thissen
an ah'll...

1998   (Cowan, '55)

       bridge over river
       bigger
            to Thorneyburn   (Common)
salmon-pools
       where otters turn

       dervish
       fools
       no more to be devilish in spate

       fate   fun

       Hadyad-Ford

(with BB)

the place had quiet when in it
only passing on the road was noise processionary
so mist was encouraged, distance discouraged
some process of time not engaged
so it was no out-of-the-ordinary
thing for otters to be breeding here again
its flatness no out of the ordinary thing
between Pennine and Hambleton hills spraint-stains
it was steady early may-time, even that not necessary:
it was the fill of the place between vague ranges
that weren't utter lines of space but own signs rearranged
receding, an approach acceding to reproach, effacing own space
headlanded with drains to field-corner pond when the pains came
she-otter ruddered from muddy-anglers'-landings
straining inland barley-beards made eyes water to shudder
heavy time of summer-not-yet but stillness goldilocks'
so blossomed as under snow but yellow focal of plain
locking marsh-sockets locating watercourses, mocking lanes
mist making parallax shift, hiding any season some of the time
low to the ground gravid stutter slow distributed sound
there might have been ferret or badger or some other critter
who would have believed the place could have stood
the rub romping cubs drubbed-ramp
or its would stir hairy-stemmed shrubs
odour oily stubends don't soil air or earth.

Vale of York 1968

(We'd been on the Tyne mouth for fish)

we watched a harbour-seal at Wylam
"there will be otters here again one day"
he remembering them in their Tyne heyday
when he was a boy. "Oh, but their *rhythm*
(the salmon and sea-trout stay, or delay
here, for the weir holds them up
and it is the first cleanish water on their way
up to the redds) "There were *redds here* in my day."
His father had one or two seals brought in, gray
and the common kind, and more often an otter
dead in nets or shot whilst at the salmon.

CS, B.B., M.P.,
1975

for Roy Laidlaw, Jed Forest

dummies the pass out, spiralling
along its axis to the hand unseen
anticipated, Rutherford at speed
we watched young otters mek snipin runs
between boulders that e'er on Rede
between boulders and alderboles in training
at dead leaves carried on current and breeze!

place this for his sniping runs
the dart that strays ahead of lang-neb
yet is of lang-neb, and ask Rutherford –
(For no other reason, the hunt comes on
the otter has won a little mere breath, this yance)

"where you've been they miss their chances
at sniping, though they have rifles they've
lost the art of hunting, are mostly for show
sounding off then the camera's on them –
yet I don't doubt their bravery in battle"*

bring it down from one range of the hill
to one gill, one borran, one birk, one lead
and lie they leaf on the ground for me!
True beauty is in such motion, emotioned
we nudge each other as the otter's wavy run
reminds of those two as one in sleet and sun –
true beauty in half-back pairing, suppose!
These stones in their intimacy roll all bones:
Coll attitiude with a rod, as God disposes.

* *(anonymous), F.C.O. '87*
with Gary Armstrong,
Rochester Transport Café 1987, revised 2001.

79

Otter, for Richard Hugo

Out of water-order otter presses shore-stones
wet chaos sprays, potters, shaking more haloes
in sunblink off sea, flank between neck, hip rudder-
pressure repeated expresses trail dark; a short trace
in time, as of vertebrae wick across Snake's slough
serpentine portage past rapids, flat curving in space
stones must be wet, states otter with every shudder
alone, even, makes toys of pebbles scatters shallows
with them, small stones must be wet to show their tones

stonks to his hover in the bark between roots and shoots
where jaw, puckered, slows, doesn't show his hand
so appearing – similar at a little distance's their oaks
ripple-ridged-rounded-crowned bank low on their boles
with deep otter pelt partly-dried, stands up from the soak
so it stood in crests and waves, grained patterns and stole
attention from each other, tho' otter seemed never still
nor is the oak now, because commotion of undergrowth
old leaves, rolled soft-grass in motion from otter flail droll

Idaho; Snake River

Martens

The Burren 1974

Three Years in Glen Garry

Three years' accounts from gamekeepers' records, an estate
kept for seasonal deer-stalking, all manner of Game preservation.
The statistics are false only in that the categories are derived
from dialect, gaelic names for fauna; they are not stories contrived...
Three hundred and seventy-one rough legged buzzards (both Buteos?)
Two hundred and seventy-five 'Kitehawks'; which might, ought,
to have included unknown amounts of various 'shitehawks'.
Two hundred and forty six martens, precious today our marten
One hundred and ninety-eight wild cats, a hundred and six polecats
– the one much reduced but recovering, the other yet to come back from the feral.
Ninety-eight peregrine falcons, six even of the Arctic gyr-falcons
seventy-eight merlins, no kestrels? (further, seven 'orange-legged' falcons)
sixty-three harriers, probably mainly hen-harriers. Ditto goshawks.
thirty-five 'horned' owls (the 'eared' species of owls, *incertae sedis*)
twenty-seven 'white-tailed' eagles (some the young, fifteen golden eagles)
eighteen ospreys, eleven hobbies; which might be average say for today.
The Clearances were not only of the people, but of most of the other indigenes
at their climax; their dynamic climax, proliferating genes
culminating food-chains, being the noblest, most beautiful, most evolved.
A country that was ours to inherit, and theirs, gone under oxters' sweep.
"Garry, stretch they bare limbs in sleep; it gars me sair to see ye weep."

nodding is trotting-on in bees, humbling
full of herself is, in the yowe-trummel

had put up little spits, bits of insects
hopping off, spiriting flitting (transects
transformed); recalling other study-district
red-stags in velvet, does slow below
stot on false-starts
flaring, their fauns running like hares,
pipit flitting collecting what a fox
put up only a few inches after apart
started stalking
                hoppers apparently,
as this mart stops, picks-up, re-starts
as physical as poetry; arising
from attentive tensions
intention and distraction-activity

sun's dull-gold shunts to vague shape
stuns, growing-old gong bringing-on
vapours groping already, going down
something so enlarged the fading hunter
less than her mirage more her 'harmony'
as of air full of itself trysting to a calm
distant mistlakes. Dissolves her cannily.

Wester Ross, Summer 1976

breath-taking you lose him
he'll not stop his 'loupin'

tho' its not so natural for him
he flattens himself over wall or rock
bough or hummock
between seaves and sedge
(without that edge of the old fox)
heather and bent-tussock
after descending fosbury-flop…

he can bleat like a lamb
or a peewit, quite as in fun,
I've not seen another lamb come
to it, nor even a peewit
nor any other bird to the spell   (has *me* well turned!)
'game' spurned, mart turns
up the wet fell, a soar
terrestrial, careless of gravity
light as a bird but big feet
caressing air, moss, grasses
stems, tail and head high, neat
the animal animated larger than life
and the easier to believe a spirit
as easily tricked us, out of sight

every snipe's scrape now, wrens curse
squirrels scold, weasel and stoat heard
like the heart swells at the pipes'
distance; as instant, for instance.

Marten-Smitt Spots

The marten's lair
not so different as our's would be, there:
Iron Age on, say; partly -underground
a "ween"   the marten-den
the route to it not direct and often
hard: the marten's way (there) insists in direction
once your eye is 'in'.

The butt-and ben
cone of debris outside   the cubs' castle
scats and midden in one, a tell-tale
the mother will often smother or carry away
and scatter, when the bracken is blessing   1959

one cub has strayed
but for this time his beauty's done the trick, the hunter
of life is its giver:
Cheryl with her
Shepherds' crook
has 'happed' him up
she's trussed him up
(his trust is up)
a week later she has shifted them all a mile up river
(*this* she, the mother...)

'The Gun', Ridsdale (1979)

'The otter has a hame in thou,
The wily fox and foumart too,
Thy rugged rocks they shelter in,
Thou bonnie, bonnie Blackburn Linn.'

"Blackburn Linn", *final verse, in* Wanny Blossoms
by James Armstrong, p. 15. 2nd edition, Hexham 1879.

Marten gait   Schubert's 5th Symphony
The Running of the Fox

from borran to burrow   red fox and red half-fox
red toad and summer-red roe   dead by the road
have only seemed so; we are the dead ones   who notice less and less as we go
though more and more is dead on the road   mustering at their same long home
to bones and stones all ground away   only messages left at cairn and gatepost:
one, injured on the Drove Road expires after managing to masticate my beef and neeps.
Dead or alive, I cannot catch him and I will not trap, but follow up to his Arnup tart
my trick only to have picked up a little of the lick, dribble of his own spittle
last week my watching brief   today less belief in my heart

as otters and foxes   many have been picked up off
roads major and minor, even car-parks   and not all had been killed by traffic.
Car-borne,   lampers kill marten crossing roads
in Northumberland   though out for poaching and for vermin
so few of these are noticed by   anyone else let alone those concerned.

'The running of the fox is nothing to the running of the mart' (J. Birkett) but the grace and speed do not save all and many are still killed including in mistake for foxes, stoats, polecats, cats and mink, to name only some. One decaying part-corpse was fished out of Cod Beck Reservoir in the late nineteen-fifties (bones in The Yorkshire Museum). I was told then that the skin had been sold in Manchester. I've heard, down the years, of several other skins going there, and to a well-known dealer in East Anglia. Few nowadays are collected by gamekeepers; the generations of gamekeepers who often felt they were obliged to make the most of such opportunities has generally passed away and in addition to that I know keepers who are seriously and genuinely interested in the welfare of these predators and the maintenance of their populations.

Chestnut(s' hissing)

This marten's standing still is hardly stillness
his dark a rhythm within him : yes
he's put on his brighter garment for the kill.
And now he is waiting where fieldfare-thrushes
come to roost dusky, as their own fading blushes.

Attentive to pigeons, or this winter's partridges?
for blood-pumps on all the ground his eye sees
are as prey to him as those are in his trees
and he is not standing still but he is planning
his dash and his kiss-at-the-neck, his prey-play
which will choke no-less-than the leopard's caress.

His running up the tree is as quick as silk
when it comes, flashes yellow breast-badge once
corkscrew ascent part of bark and branch
its crown Scots pines-rudding yet, or of that ilk.
Long time in the tree, and we neither hear nor see
whether it is a pigeon that returns him from trance
invisible to us again; in no disturbance.

with Margaret, Upper Teesdale, 2002

Starling, when it is almost over,
starting at the presence of the marten
our field-flow of thought for
we expected the one only when the other
(not noticed either) (they are not apart,
were not, in our awareness) our hearts
jump; tho' startings have them harder.

We are on a line when things can
come, clarify, put together gradually.
The old marten-masters, willy-nilly
with the few present day ones span
marten matters best.
Infinite waiting deceives
except the marten, at rest.

He has taken the windrow at a run
without stopping somehow (he) will look you in the eye
rest of his form unexpectedly near or surprisingly far away.

Suddenly, then, on us, over us, past us, under us
the eye wanders a range of blunders over the early years
back of the eye the other matters are
seen not to matter; not disillusion
the marten, as if dog, wanders off
on his own round of checking, in time
foreign to us. There are other things for that eye
and the other; a few for them both together
the secret of good adjustment is to be doing
something you don't see until you see it again
dew to rain to river to response quite other;
who of us can say we gave the hunter or the hunted
his chance, which variables in the equation
let alone other individuals, other animals.

falling-over notes and   unravelling marvelling
of such terrifying weather   tumbling around the fellsides
marten suffers travail in such storm, having to travel
with ewes windraked   behind their dykes
and rabbits blinded   blasted by dry blizzard
as the Helmwind blazes   drily all before it
physically assailed   "the devil is behind it"
waster, wave wind   of pure wall-force
laid on, burnished-blue   barrels brown-bracken
spoils spirals spout   whaleback 'banks'

         — such clouds as are   night emphatic not to be lifted
but to be pressed in to brass rubbings by this heavy drubbing
sifting in to the soil horizon next under the tormented surface
hammered heavy, but feverish of its hammered-finish
gunbarrel-blueing not to be lifted by any sort of morning
sun or given the life of rust, rive skinned of rind
twisting in release, fraying in this cold, stunning
a violet-coil had dried to a spring springing in minutes
the gentlest thing, scat to collect it in that violence
fossil, some ammonite stone silence in the cabinet.

Black Sail Y.H. 1960
revised Garrigill 1994

Great Lakes Woods

marten the leopard of mustelids
with fisher the complete predator
eyelets all the little lake-inlets
thread beside otter and mink, not
fisher here. As drawn to fishing spots
as to my smelt laid down as bait.
Five miles inland the same family

Five miles away the same martens
dam and three kits three months old
have emptied a tree of chickadees
roosting there together, up twenty feet
and out on fine twigs, unbroken.
We watched by moonlight nightsight
the slightest kit had nipped all ten.

Hiawatha National Forest
1973-76

A way of martens through trees

Diddering earwhisk antennae, shoulder-blades,
otherwise nothing but a stir-wryneck, shades
tail carried low behind, legs folded – under
mostly. I supposed all this low-profile for
contour of the beech branch progress, and wonder

nature is never abstract only idea
and hope. Stars hard work, to steer.

the way of a marten in a tree, in trees
is not the way of a squirrel, not that ease
and lightness, though if you see martens first
(few do?) you could be excused of such pride
as ever is before a greater game is realized

we are come home, we the watchers watched
as ever we cross over or are crossed over to
and some impatience scotched (again) new   (rebate tossed and)

No, the way of a marten in trees is *with* trees
he's using the trees, manipulating some forces
breaking some twigs – as you have to break eggs
– some forces *they* have, as well as his own ones
learned – he's had to learn and some do not do well...

Infinitude, the multitude in a tiny lined view   (section, trued)
kaleidoscopes nature with man and only two
elements depend so on each other.

The way of a marten in trees is no pinnace in seas
that squirrels can seem, even dormice at their scale:
is bewildering if there is a chase: it is speed
it is confusion of limbs, and skill and risk
after a moment you realise some will quite fail

the meanest worm can squirm into our aimless aim-
drying-out on our stretch of road in the rain we passing
and again we are connected. But *this* is a noble moment!

the way of a marten in trees, teaching its kittens
is still, say, as good as a cat, a wildcat, a stoat
but the kittens, like otter cubs in their elements
are slow learners and will be very slow earners
if they have to live by the birds or nests they can reach

we are home but find it even stranger than before
an unwalked shore higher, effort renewed; and desire

C.S. to B.B., in litt. *1978*

(Northern Ontario Jan 1976)

Round the clock, for the sky's show
silences, mocks, brings (out) on to the snow

where again I tried leaving
honey-jars out on the ground
some of them tied to a branch,
wide-mouthed enough; only a little
honey or maple syrup in any one,
old preserved fruits, blue-berry jam
a trapline for me also; the spittle
making.
        seven-mile snowshoe round
jack-pine to muskeg, kettles' edge
more thirst than cold at thirty below
stripped sedge fractures script the way to go

waiting on each place according to
wind and scent; attention settled,
mind hunts across, fording divisions
affording visions needing as much sight
searching inward for what there *was* :
this Evening Grosbeak, that Hawfinch
al*low*ed their marten. Equally slow reactions,
pine siskin shouting over each incident;
spruce grouse heads only showing
(red grouse at home) (above the snow
blackgame feed at just such slows
just such dusk.)
        Another marten rushes
at Siskin, killing without breaking lope
only yards away the squirrel can cope
unperturbed with his cone; this time rising
sun blushes whiskey-jack witness
confidence in his cursing-fit grows
not a marten-broken item shows.

One gin trap less

left in gin jaws most of forelegs
cut free by his own
persistent gnawing

the dog would soon have
followed-up the remainder
but I, already in the wood
trod in the marten blood

yet had not the trail
darkened the leaves further by
draggle bruise, and early flies
I might yet have failed
to find the marten in time

Even so the   brains
had already been taken away
with most of the head
a fox indicated by scent stains
and two full miles away
towards the den I had been
approaching that April day
anyway, now heavier.

Crows had riven
corbies, daws or rooks
cut at the shoulders' open stumps.
Mart, dead of fox
maimed by a boy
to sell his skin for cartridges
(told of how slow mart had died
in own shit, toyed with his pie;
and asked me why I'd given him it)

a 3lb animal;
I salvaged most of the skin.

Northumberland

The Weasel of Great Smeaton

"If it crosses your path, look out for bad luck in love"*

It came out of the dubbs
on their breath of evening
a habitat at once favoured
in such as East Anglia
thus unexpected in the North
though at least in Sutherland
and the Merse

"weasel" is the whole tribe in dialect
diatribe, all tarred with same brush
penetrative an organ through
the short grass skirts of life, not love

pencil, long very penetrative powers
I bonnet long   edges
rend, run as a stoat between hedges

the modern car
has finally achieved its utter carnal
banality of life, and of ways of death to go with it
of incontrovertible in convertible intent
surrogate and desertification inside and out
Motorcars so hot to touch because they've spurned the sun
as fully as any weather   anywhere they come
recoil upholsters   curved-scratches in the polish of a gun
to our violence swinging at our hip   unzipped ex-hipsters

(1973)

* *G. Palmer and N. Lloyd: 'The Obstinate Ghost and other ghostly tales'. London, Odhams 1968 Ch.3, pp 39-44*

and I've heard similar legends in the N.W. of England, and the Pacific N.W

We live in all around us, Joy

Two days' snows never the same; two hours marten-watching
themes reported repeated on varied vortices, themselves revealing
successions responding to representing, reciprocating as if those individual
conifers tide and wood rack of the forest's edge-effect defecating
these coils violent violet vibrant ejecta, and what did any but squirrels
dropping it say of the cone, that it had come down on us, was, a swirl

The clearings, glades and the planned-to-provide-firebreak rides
tunnels of greater and greater gloom through the afternoon, and less room
in no relation to the slopes; so that bad windblow windrowed soon
also reflecting fallen whose tumuli being also rockfall – rooks
no headstones and buried long ago, when and where these forces decide.
The marten died in Wyoming over Grosventre twenty years ago
because of its interest in, involvement in, just such long late snow
falling, we are living not as to ourselves but as to such once ones
in part, part in inevitable self-consciousness raises us and an awareness
with the snow fall and the dark closing in and off all northern-ness.
Not needing the avalanche, not heeding it if it comes and fills full
us a few more minutes, maybe than that watched marten had then.

Feb 4, 1996

Kits at Midden:

Dead-litter about martenden
– red mouthline, pink and madder
(amber underside of adder)
– kits rustle, rattle as dry rusks
larch bark sheaths, beech husks
teeth – score on them, worry away
"lift" and "tip-cat" flurry of play

(Marten and Lizard
moved on after
more sheep to come)

growing   load
thick gravid lizards as
thinly trailed along the wall
periwinkle watching
grooved   wood
turnings   (in our road)
goad   the eye

stood the little bottle
found that day, may have been
Roman
between the Cottonshope and Chew Green
in a raffia of grass frass older
than the turves over

marten tripped and traipsed
fence a periphery of vision
being wire. Wound nest
above rare here, redstarts',
lately grown undergrowth, zest
taken as en passant as choice
wild raspberries six weeks on

now all but the fencepost gone

1975, 1989

The soil no longer soil
and that infracture
of a thousand woods
and woods on woods had gone

He'd seen something like it
with blood and bandages
and a cloud of smell
on smell that hung about

'Happy' to shovel it
still getting back into trenches
at Ypres of
beyond. The same moonlight.

The concrete clay hung
to the marten's paws
all that night
he watched.

M6 motorway; the Navvie's memory (c1969)

sun soft as ease
quiet seas   enlarged, strowing
shims out stripes   widening these trees
halowing
your hair
putting me in mind of
curls, curlicues, ringlets off the Indian's
cutting cottonwood-stem   its chips and
dust flying
marten looking-on
moth waiting for evening
on the same bark the marten clasps
not as the squirrel does
more as the wind
and the wind off his scent
and off yours.

Is the only tree taken
for the village   for ceremony
the marten shifts for the breeze
the man apologises to the trees   and this
tree   the sun
cloud and he wipes off

long after he went the West is

marten moving on, for early berries
cherries beginning to repeat the sun
run, the last song, father of the silence

June 73 Wyo / Montana
June 96 North Pennines

7 May 1987

(disappointment the inappropriate
emotion registered at the marten)

on a rootplate at the sudden swivel
dead rootlets rotate resisting perception
of commotion emergent Red Squirrel

frozen a second as if caught in the open
equal materialisation from the bracken
a pylon emergent from fog only at moment
of frizzle over him; a cross-over flashing

Marten into the path the squirrel lept
yards bounded alongside well into the open
before the tap-tackle breaking its neck
at the run like that fisher hit marmot
stunned, stopped, corralled and roped-in

away wavy hair-grass dragging at reins
scruff of the neck as if pulling kits
grunts as if at them but at it, kill
the brains sucked in, under the fell-gate
away, leaving the rest. The rest of the day
I stay, just in case, happy unknown to wait

Aeolian

for J.U.

breath rhymes • scent of thyme on even air
off gillside • soft violets line chimes • meaner there
(hardly a whiff of them, at the best of times)

such humid days • after there's been some sunshine
(especially before thunder rolls down off the fells)
even *our* noses can pick up vole, grouse smells

so what for the marten timing his threshold airing
upwind of the fox; his den-entrance parabolic
to steady sunshift, breeze out of any warmer quarter

no wonder he'll dance, as if still a kit; run, frolic
onto scree below, heatherbrae-brim above; the bracken
(between green hooks yet) will dull even that glint of water
and its roar which fills • long after storm-grumbles slacken.

June 1997

He came on a second; and, after, the fox;
making his run through the wood,
one maybe for his life. He existed
anyway for me only a pulse in my blood
treeing the squirrel I hadn't noticed...

I dug on. Upturned rows show lightening
the sky is making morning
certain work only, and slow
– oh, cold spray off the sliced-turfs shaking
blued spade chucks up around ears; shocks onto neck!
Hill mist drifts last from the trees and their gill
my smoke starts straight, to obscure them again
and they are burning the heather on the rim ring of hill
to be more sure of day than anything might still.

Woodhead 1984 (March)

Cisa Appenina between Milan and Pisa
Coretta between Pisa and Bologna
Futa between Bologna and Firenze

The River Magra separates the Ligurian Alps
from the Ligurian Appenines by either of two passes:
Cadibona (calcareous to the west,
schists and marls and grits to the east)
or Goia Pass between Satona and Genoan Alps
Appenine/Alpine roadpasses Gilera'd (All-State)
Appenines and Antiappenines form one nappe
nights napped in the snow: machine frosted over
camp inspection by martore

Ducati 340 }
Gilera 125 }
1972

American Marten in Northumberland
discovered, living wild and little-known, 1969-70

From the front, they walk a waddle or a limp,
from the side you see the foot go down gently, quickly, flat,
a short shuffle forward (deceptively enough)
just like real Red Indians, hardly making a stir.

You distinguish these from ours by their white faces,
reddening the bracken where 'keepers shot ours out'
undulating into that same receptive sunset
such that they are not there,
something to do with flow.

Brutalised by our streets and shoes
we stumble after their gap in our long disengagement.

Long-tailed weasel
                    cheetah swagger
jaeger jaguar
                long-tail hunters
twist pursuit swinging laterally
              wavy-chasers
otter and not only in the watter

tail as brake, rudder
              marten

U. Pen. Michigan 1973

(from some Welsh fieldwork)...

...before I know, I'm picking up particular pattern
I'm picking up that pattern of sense and on memory
familiarity is in, and in more than, comfort of an old tune
against other noises in the same darkness,
picking up that smother of 'noise' in her precise reception
the jill-marten pattering sure – there is yet no moon;
improvising on, and now improving on, my own rhythm
making this my passacaglia, as it is her part-pavement
regular a few minutes, a night, or a winter season
– forty years of this, (and more) different places; only a part
so that I pick up slow marten footfall against leaf fall
more on this air than on my idea, more than I know
and I mutter as she does, sing under my breath and heart
response no matter how foolish, totter toward its art...

Berwyns, 1995/6

Starting the Night-shift

19/20 Oct 2000
for M.H.

Dusk weasel, gone to bed after Kestrel
both after Starlings bushed, uselessly
whistle of wigeon over the river
under Mars, Saturn rising under Jupiter
(Orion not yet up over horizon)

Eighteen blackcock to roost, where they lekked
"lookin' for their likin'" on same urges
flown-in from their Leadgate road herb-verges
whimpers the dog-marten toward 'em corralling,
forward at an easy, not a dog, trot, silhouette

Eighteen blackcock in a loose circlet of jet,
lyre-tails lean inward - no white show, give away,
no white also my facing them, not the moon's yet
light seeks these high sikes from the west
red-coral while sunset delays over Solway.

Isn't Listening

brushing the window hail electric
contacts make-and-break arcuate
current in both of us, breath intake, (hissing)
hearing and watching is still missing
whatever it is we could eventually say
"she's back again, she's back again"
preposterous tail, – gloss glistening

"*He's* near as big as the vixen"
this beech wood yielded to the hunt
– "but she, she's canny, mebbe the runt…"
'when fox is scarce, marts is mair'

Then a wild squall, and that is all
rain on the west-wind's winter flail
"when we'd expected snow to fall".

Woodhead
20/21 Dec 1989

(Male martens have 'rests':
'hovers' they revisit passing through)

rocks, ground-shelter most and easiest
but least-found; this Scots pine-top proud
grown-out is cradling a marten's nest:
and an old red squirrel drey, a goldcrest's...
—even the new spruces have them, north and west.
...shocked at the shake in it, calling out loud
than panic at the unexpected directly overhead
snow and ice cascade as noisily instead
at the marten's restless-settling, turning tight
on his own tail, as a cat will for the night
denying, coming-on, all winter in that cloud.

in the broken lands of the Ketilness
clay-chobbers (dry, crumbs) tumble
old jet and alum mines, quarries' mess
ironstone taken off, batts of it; a jumble
of old workings marking massive erosion
of inland and coast, masking casual destruction
where the hunted marten a minor occasion

wildcats once, and foxes ever and anon
all one then. Since the eighteen-forties
few martens and probably no true cats
bar the feral kind; a situation repeated
in broken reefs of the limestone far inland
the juniper woods' that were and a few still are
the gill woods' and fell-lands' "sanctuary"

the same old-timer who had told me of
and taken me to "Beowulf's" Boulby
great beast cliff, and lesser Beast Cliffs (along
by the Cat-Trod paths and the cliff-tops')
one night but we saw no marten nor even fox
yet in the sea caves a seal cub in the rocks
where he'd expected we might find an otter.

Oct 1958

Running wick, leaping, loping "sent"
Smaller, yet taller in the excitement
'Like the fox' is not what I meant
blent, his trails away from denouement
he is too big for Chamber Music
and an animal of astonishing beauty

marten ranges as widely as does otter
the branches sway after his detachment
avalanches a little snow down
precipice of ice crystals scatter from
his running through the burran, fluid

has put a tune in the drumming wind
his running over the bare rock clitter
leaping and finding again immediate traction
marten expands and contracts with action

Feelings raised by the way things went
world stops turning for such a moment
which started on a note of presentiment

In full sail before the wind, flags unfurled
I, also, want to perch lightly on the world
its rim; no less less lightly than a bird
but I am a cross-fox heafed on my hill

and in, across and under the trees
only ever is this passage visible
for a few seconds, a proportion,
speed decreased, at *his* ease
spurning my stumble and I've lost him
but for a few dead leaves still falling
a jay along his way – warning calling

"Lucky you got that skin; good news!"

No, Terry, that marten-skin
is not 'good news:'
it is one less of the kith and kin
north country 'true'
not, evidently, ranch-derived stock
(how many are?);
and gone to the car, not even the gin.

How many deaths go unrecorded?
– its neither relief nor recompense
that this one passed for 'a stoat'
when the major stopped after it
cast it over the fence, and wall;
(just where those who had robbed his hall
had hidden some loot to be found by us…)

but only 'lucky' in that one can
guess a little better at their span:
this one Lesley and I had watched
cross the road at this same spot
(another night, an otter did…).
Each such incident, and this is best
indicates ignorance; and all the rest!

(at the same spot a few years earlier a well known 'environmentalist', not knowing the road, had killed a gravid red squirrel; as he admitted, easily avoidable, with his car)

in litt. *to T Coult, mid December 1993 [a corpse salvaged]*

Mart out of the trees beneath the thistles

I spoke to MacDiarmid
he deploring the skin-trade
he told me still operated
in Scotland "on some estates"
the Martens, in their richesse
are for adoration, athleticism…
I agree on a certain this-ness
the marten as exuberance
but not, not that old chestnut
a figure of self; self-expression
that unacceptable indulgence…

The whisky warmed. My predation
his thistle as symbol of non-self
of absence of self. Of the country
his poem of the thistle a celebration
of the descent to earth, speed, space
with a hint in it, more than a hint
and to someone more than I was then
a distinct sense of his status in it.
Our Gaelic and Siberian reference   *showing him skins*
at one remove Scots, Amerindian   *of martens, 1976*
totemic, not commercial, dissonance.   *at Biggar.*

March nightsweat, wondering where winter went
stopped midstride for a marten scent late last lent
over her prey in a field improved-ley, above the Lune.

Watched again June, mimicking a cat at a mole
as grey as its many little hills, the whole grown grey
by dawn. Her den, and my bed only minutes away
we slipped away satisfied, reddening, alone, more whole

Marten, anchored into tree
kedges best the tail against
gale, which takes selectively

hail spots her nape and mantle
she's more shaken by missel–
storm and rant at her ettle
eggs still warm each pouched
in her eyeshrunk grin; two left.

Finned around pale bole old cottonwood
as she descends after the thunder
pressed against or because of the wet
tail short, but between friction
brake and prehensile contraption
stopped my blood contour hugging yet
shed, all in one movement she's up
cupping something under her chin
on her hindlegs and rudder-prop
scorching me, lets the egg* drop...

* Grey Heron

Tarset 1956
Washington State 1973

Castoring swivels big at ends of legs
wrist-slips away from whelps
starts over swidden
at risk; first-light in the open
why then posturing apparent, intent
stretching all ways, at the summit
Banktop; taking-the-airs, in fact.

Shawled in her own warm energy
casting airs, cannot be cooped-up
wick as all weasels, "bonning-oop
tahm, gates we cannut glim or grip"
(attitude, energy her synergy for the hunt).
An hour at this front, catch and carry in one
movement lizard out in the sun to hazard
back to the den – easily missed buffets in heather:
"should be stooked in such weather."

April 1971
North York Moors

scuffle at the double, Little Jack Russell
at the dyke prrrs   rrrr   sstinnn
all night the marten's laffin   fussin.
These martens this summer; young wouldn't come
nearer me than their mother
the mother whickers and the kits come to heel
unwilling to come out onto the dew

once, shirt off, midday in the sun
they were more awake than I was

Redesdale May'86

The day proved almost same gloom
grain of fell felled in the dark
wavelength overlengthening then.

a mite's bite in a slice
sun upcome focussed on,
same eye or hearth breast breathed
yellow-rouge marten's badge,
blossom or berry (rowan) bright.

greens of the place laced, though,
glowed on their own light despite
lightening ever for old seed-heads
levelled, then began to leach
under the same sun steadied them.

I'd found the den overnight
nervous on its little shifts of wind
which filter the fell incompletely
as the fell its stars time spinned
not the same stars, marten, next time.

stain at the midden, hidden in sky
enough bidding and temporary
transient as the next day's lie
is this one's, and as wary
of showing a rhyme, or line.

Nov. '78

Marten are in the ruined biggin
on the fellside, where the smell changed
and the jackdaws nest no more, this spring
squabs were cleaned out still in the nest
til all were gone, visit after visit,
by the hungry bitch feeding young; next spring
her young did tumble, King-of-the-Castle.

Marten, 1991
Northumberland

Only showing as dark wing-brushes
blotches, the owl turns the woodend
tearing calico off snowdust thrushes
missels the marten is nervous at as
a cat, leaps light tight on to our lean-to
tilts the clear snow, where even a cat
wouldn't go, up the eaves-stones sloped
steep, once to hold the old heather-thatch
goes through the one tile-gap on a lope
to where woodmice winter on beech mast
and our ungathered-in plums, cheese-crumbs

explosion second, pheasant's slow rocket
(ballista no more so, or trebuchet)
but one squawk shortened at throat
impetus aborted as suddenly as a shot
serpent flung at, clings on, redcoat
on gawdy, tangle as wrestling adders
– more vigour – both suffusing redder
hillmist hare's-tail bruised to madder
already begins the marten-paw ploat
before the bird is dead of his suffocations
wings fling a shiver, silvered leg tendons.

Woodhead 1988, 1991.

Marten at Rydal

for the jays.

Freezing of commotion spoke of movement.
Yet all the corner of my eye returned
(short emotion before the second look was spurned)
was insufficient message to brain. That moment
we sensed a little more than what we saw –
the deadfern fronds as Marten turn and burn.

Seeing not all, we were observed entire
as if out that beechbole the all-seeing
suddenly made us flush hot, of simply being
as caving collapse of wood brings rudd to fire.
Stance was stiffened as he raised his rough paw
hesitant the standstill he turned to flee.

Motoring scree, muttering energy,
marten, with as much carelessness and joy
and wander as the football-dribbling boy
left the wood-brushed crags to you, to me
rejoicing new store of fruit, and another door
opening into nature, and for memory.

1956
Rev. 1970

for Bill Swallwell
(the Thirlmere Pipe)

Walking and working the many miles all weathers
a natural man in his awareness of nature
he loves the Lake Hills for the life they showed him
ever on the pipelines from Thirlmere, the New Lake
for the Manchester Water Works.
He had asked me directly what it was I looked for
so repeatedly, and after weeks I told him, showed him
paw prints and scats; later photographs of "the mart".
He drew me ears, tail, loop, foot fur every other 'part'...
and a skull in his Grasmere council house's outside privvy.
Over the years, and from others, he had saved three
would give them to Tullie House one day, he told me...
with another skull or two of fox, and of badger
another he had (he'd seen others) was of a bitch otter

for H. Gilonis   **Burren, Martens 1**

[After basket of eggs topography under basket of eggs skies]

     windroll and cloud roll
     as limestone – rands at home   (feeling at home)
     hummocks, hammocks, ribs and knolls -in-rows.
     In a land on
     winds way
     waving and rolling as the sea beyond
     so near as to
     shift mood
     repetitions   represent the bounding of a marten
     wavy breeze   excitement   lifts
     sunset net rude   under and into tilting trees

Toolin near Dooler 1960, 1988

Burren, Martens 2

Martens in a high wind, as in Northumbria,
line-astern avoiding, in their rhythm, waving branches and
if they are whickering I cannot hear them; no sense of hysteria!
cobbles scampering clints and grykes seems to wobble this one mossy mass
raft of limestone toppling   tumbling leagues
depopulation after the Famine, a geometry   reckless rockfall
Knockasin and Cattlekinch
          spirits den under chockstones
                    Ballyvaughan rhythm the tilt, the three Aran Islands (offshore)

(July 1960)

**(Mart
– with Beryl**

listen like each other

while windsquall sounds
chimneys organs around
these crags I wonder
at you consciousness (turning)
of it the pass its passacaglia
over into the sour milk ghyll
we are high-strung together

will we reach a point of gain
conscious experience in the brain
(again, of such as martens'?)
consciousness as unitary for them
as it is for us, as particulate
particulars obviously differ
no doubt every way, rhythm

with what joy to find one
in this same cleugh near Ewe Hill
where as a boy *ah fund yan*
(yeears after, the seame thrill
– first, bein' shown a marts kill
for the first tahm) these shits
spill o' rowanberry goo drittle

mebbe as sore in their bellies
as they have been in ours
(even as jam and tart and beer
and wine) – but that day we
ate them because of the marten –
and you hevving to piss your wellies
on the red United 'bus home!

(S. Grillo, Brenda Richardson)

just as there'd been dormice twice
over the same years as hers, and hers
other black-eyed berry for these girls'
first clue to presence there – don't err
either, familiar blackberries, 'brambles'
best in some brakes the marten takes
as two of us, years ago, best blaeberries
cleared out before our learning eyes
not forgotten, either, purpled muzzle
nearly as dark and liquid, mobile,
clear trail stained dew and drizzle.

Antelope Marten Antelope Flats (Wyo '97)

Jake, stake skins on it
forelocks nothing so soft
black curls rocking daft
gypsies' parting shocks
shake on shift and farting
marten lugs and whiskers
reductio ad absurdum:
only just not rocked when
they coughed or at that
tail-flick, longer swish
which is the give-away
marten, otter, the big cat
mocking buttes stately *at*
the point of recognition

Abrupt up from the Hole
sagebrush stains delicate
range after their noses whole
antelope. Pronghorn dilate
(the newspaper wallpaper
lining the cabin palimpsest
collage as their breath.
Harmony these acceleration
coats as close a harmony
heraldic as in pavilions
(the National Wildlife Museum)
in the same flashing from motion
marten runs at the starlings
out of the trees, bison-attendant;
red brown, cream white as these
pronghorns at similar speed

March 20;
Cuddy's Day

Snow snaps at the face
their faces. They gnaw
at it, their breath their
nerve melts. One claw
scratches skin for flesh
with a peculiar grace
which stops the whole show
and I feel more, more nesh
than I can say, or know.

The joy of living is partly this and thus

you can bound over the rocks
loose and sharp, marten and fox
not caring where you put a foot

we are as planned for the hunt
when the blood is up, shoot
secondary to chase, and love
is in it, of *it*. Close as a glove;
and to be hunted and the less and loss
not being hunted, not feeling *it*.

Feb 1st 1998

Marten at pheasants two
coming-up behind them
in the manner of cats yet
foot by foot stalk slow slew
approximate, less 'interested'
seven foot behind minutes and then
rise and dash throwing all eight
feet bolas : one or two wrap *la*te
round each pheasant one leg
up on their tarsi, wings spread
winded before the bite to the neck
the impetus rolling all over and over
as after goshawk strike at the head
blackbird alarms only after they're dead

ripples renew through the wood
on the hill beyond, over from the wall
late-dawn grey pink then blood
rims hill-line fades and dims
still as the noise has, no flood
of light. The brightest glow all
in the pipe bowl before the drag
leads, old leaf reds, one trail
feathers on the morning flag

Least-weasels not so soft in tones
run arctic vole holes between the feet
we muskeg, as if they had no bones...
the hallucinations: the   loneliness
and the sudden utter (hysteric?) deceptiveness
of the growing glowing light and dark
of the freezing instant air on air as mist
hoar, as in the arctic distant outcrops
prove, a few steps further on
pieces of rock you could pass from hand to hand.
Because their ears are so large
martens become wolverines, half way to bears
their bounding, fur up, yet squeezing through
into consciousness of what they suggest not true
they are no more than polecats or great stoats
a few steps further on.
Because their eyes are so large, their ears so round
you can't believe when they've gone to ground

Marten lit
middle of wet
where we'd not
even seen it
sways away
little russet bull
all chest and chunter
little red adder
had copied his
sinuous motion

    ..

tree waves
energy saves
a marten for
running them
their harmony.
Trees reflect a
wind of their own
related to it
light change
also, same wave
reveals rime
in them all
the whole scene
the only time

    ..

not the wave
form of roe
nor the sound
in the ground
over it all
deer s*tall*
at the halt

the squirrel
another rhythm
down is near
(non mustelid)
tumbling-in
not the waterform
of roe or waterfall
watermark mart

Marten deceives his pursuer (me...)

snap-on head that fills exactly
voles – or that wall's long-hole
where it goes the rest of him can follow

and laughed at the naturalist
because his life has bitten through
bookbinding, paper and glue

licked the blood of author, authority
official and monitoring busy body
snagged on barbed wire a clue...

'we' wrote his premature obituary
over and over again, if we believed it
declared him ripe for re-invention...

reintroduction is. On our terms, then
but he won't have *our* own terms
even if we have to rub him out

sadness not in it: laugh at him
and salute survivor *or* extinction
it is *his* way we only stumble at

the fields, neat and productive
will know him again, or do so now
enlarged for his, not our, (re)creation

The marten comes up, with the otter
it's only for them, their *next* generation
before they will 'disappear' again!

Nov. 3

she missed her dawn run
at rabbit; last urge
of long night on frost
they'd seen her targe
or had her scent or heard
her drum, roll down the fell
one stone run on further than
the others spilled insolent
frost loosened the gill

little thunder, lost when
the burns were up, stuns
even her balanced walk, run
and shuffle; about seven
syllables and she's half
a furlong, a hundred yards
about only four scarf-
waves of her tail forwards
pauses on her two centres

one or two stones rocked
once; wren, silent, tail-cocked
shocking is so I take the blame
after all, now it is the same
whether the one intruder or the other
rehearses the confidence of shelter
within, winter and wall-walk on
tups sigh, higher yowes cough wait on:
none-hunting marten must have gone

Nov 14 1997
Eden

after full moon light night fine dawn
red-ragged clouds down in the east
its wind under helm bar blasts west
a few small gooseflights skeining gain
height in the clear between bar and roll
watched by the jill marten; tail drawn
off the frost on the dyke. Ice gone
by nine a.m., but not from the shadows
she denned in where I found the racloir
or whatever it really is, in seventy-four
(and the last time 1 saw a marten so slow...

Marten and Otter
(CS/BB/?NN)
(by Birk Bridge, Duddondale)

"Nights solo spent in hoggarths above here"
CS found an otter in one, once,
        asleep on a hot afternoon

                surprisingly, like the otters
                the martens have the power, the gall
                to utterly disappear from in front of us
                as if they'd never been here at all!
                But you do remember the hour they were
                as (often) at the sunstall behind the hill
                when awareness, and time stood still

Knowing (where)
to turn by the becks'
the burns' turbine
noting   signals
the watters rise and fall
not the same as
their calling
(to an otter)

Mart, between squirrel-tail, puma-tail
cheetah impetus, speed-cheater: all swivel and shake
tailswing in twist-chase   is rudder   and brake
– the long-tailed hunter's extra grace
                                        a balance make
(phalanxes of parallel note   teeter to(ward) notion

Otterrudder   not only for parting of water
(but) utterly effective   blunt   shudder
 stuns   runningrabbitscut   deliberate
cutting a swathe through   bruising   ideas of predation
(and) lizard's, his is   busy (h)is   passing   (c)litter
in dead brown-leaf-litter   whin furze
                                    but mere whif(t) of whistle
hunting the spider in sticks of smooth Melancholy-thistle
MacDiarmid and Bunting, in whisky, yet not missed-him
or his running, our fun directed by his fun
three men on the lonnen   after booze at the Dragon

Upper Peninsula Michigan '73, '75
Cumbria '75, '76

It was, I suggested
Bulls in the Afternoon

she agreed, the meek
but strong old Brigantian
widow who had read
Ernest Hemingway
(and *only* him, she said)

She found the first marten
cubs to be seen (for so long
in the vice county, over
a century anyway) *so far
as we know*, at least
by a naturalist, that is...
and *drew* them in the dark

Marten rising

(Constellation once)
                        the sun
whose splendour levels at evening
reddens the pine stems the reddening
rushstems harestails aglow, stunning

chooses red squirrels poised an ideal
aflame consuming shades in the wood
and bringing-on others and the near wall
faces and the further mountain-wall
stand red in stone as if of live blood
rubbing air to electric, aeolian
music, brings-on the night to fall
of the red fox, red owl, and marten

The moon at its brightest
these hours, they tell us
for a hundred and thirty three years
– must their eyes be logarithmic as ours?
or might it be even brighter for these?

When whin's blooms out of sight
when whin has not yellow showing
love's been forgotten, out of fashion
their points, distant zones, are glowing
the marten's way and mine all night.

1999

144

Marten Hunting

Like the mink I've also seen use them slip
through difficult peat, old bog, at their wettest
seen less likely while he uses the gripps
and the sikes; sic dirrect-running trips
can be a mile and more, even the deep-
plew in the forest, tunnels in summer
as in the rides, we can anticipate his angles
cut-corners, portages, often avoiding being
'scented' even, and seen: but these runnels
hide him shadow and overhang and sway
are communication-trenches. Don't give him away.

Our hope dangles and hangs on chances
– not often the badger-trod predictability
and don't resent it. He *will* hunt paths
and scavenge roads, but his hunting ability
is so various I am a t a loss, and in ignorance...
a number of them make useful transects
these nets of gripps and little burns and sikes
like otter he'll carrion from lambs and any
other fallen stock, even like foxes rob
the keeper's gibbets, even the hill farmer's
lines of moles along the wire on the dykes

Upper Lunedale
to Swaledale
1980

A day I didn't see marten   (1981)
I started at their being there

scent the most direct sense
and the most profound for sense
dense in the swallowing even in
ignorance; no doubt so to marten
badger, otter, weasels, wolverine
and even we can catch a hint
consciously, less alone the unknown
to us yet. Hippocampus is in
from the snout and so straight
to inevitable internal slate
unknowing external states may miss...

so also I wear the same clothes
on the trail for the same individual
(though I fail to remember often enough)
by the same route, so the residual
traces I lay are part of the same stuff
I am, what I eat, hum, so that
if I smell marten, whistle; pattern
can assert itself from me: to me
perhaps if I am lucky, the poem
if is does not have to make sense –
I'd be suspicious if it did, of myself

then the associations, around discoveries,
some of the connections, even reveries
themselves recognition, acknowledgment
way crosses way we came and went
something will stay for the merriment
the thanking of nature, the creator
as beyond nature as there in her.

Batting at Hawnby
I was more or less useless
and at Wass 'half-asleep'
"but scoring, as usual, is
canny, bats too timidly."
Bowling at Oldstead's
no better, but *fielding*
now there I was *happy*
I would patrol the deep...

The other boy-gamekeepers
'apprentice' with Thompson
and Gordon or Close. "Sleepers,
'carried' by the rest of the lads"
really. Hardly any unison
with the bowlers and far away...
innings that lasted all day!

But we filled score-cards complete
match after match; full of interest
birds and beasts watched closely,
more or less, from the boundary:
even sketches at times, replete
with diagnostic features: already
the hawks, the weasel family and,
by far for us then the best,
once the "clubster wi sic girt feet!"
He left such a wake in the dew
just then fallen, Brian, for me and you
and better than Dave's half-a-century!

(He wanted to give his Army compass
  to me, but I persuaded him not)

magnet enough the College Burn otters
the Pillar Rock martens of his boyhood
for me to find direction, metal partial
and we to prefer Cheviot and Tarset
and Cross Fell to Mallerstang, Warcop
Hunderthwaites' shelf fell full of martial
he'd say marching song though laverock's

Lodola's lullaby croons on the overrun
Raven's and big Brough's idle grumble
his glissade of Langdales' scree-run
my axe-rough and Meldon's crumble
recalled at the fireside, splitting kindling
offset and counterpointed by anything
we'd start from the pipits and hill-wren.
Caught in the graticule on Simonsides
girls in the gillsides laughing in ling
red marten ran for them, otter whistled again –
goodwill in gratitude shaking his sides!

'He' is Basil Bunting.

148

Marten, North Riding Coast

about cliff wykes   gills-in
bracken, bramble and alder marten
the bolder marten abreast the squalls
along Beast Cliff, Yat o' the storms
Northsea, nor'easter familiar this
elder marten the mair pale, toward
sandy pelage, faded moult after moult
old-carpet, brush flash, a touch fresh
of pink-glowing warms as of flesh
as lowering (sun)light flanks bleached
lank legfur feathers as it dries on
flashing white about breast and gills
spills downbreast the old milkstain
bib of fur thinning, thrill distills

grown to love the grey mornings
and the long wet grey evenings
rigid darkness nights as empty hard
as pencils of car-lights and the stark
disturbances of distant bare house lights
distracting, destructive of vigil
and chase, relentless rain is
not charmless, silver the way is

1955 (rev. 1999)

(Sister)   Jean, Rockies 1973

Like a kiss burns it is equinox's promise
the vigor of cloudshift, wind turn, mixes
of light and wet and dry that raze or rasp
the skin and lift an expectation, as pollen fixes
life a moment; there he is gone away again
less substantial, as silent as scream of vixen
is silent rehearsal silhouette wind dispersal
bark of fox we (also) miss when somehow his grasp
comes on the place, displaces hers, district a night or two
a few days, even a week; as when otters come through
as if other things held their breath is stayed out of sight
– unexpected and undemonstrative, to us, dominance reversal
less obvious than observed: of trees, of glances moonlight
breath is held for the marten present, current demersal.

When I see the lift of his tail-tip, the prick of his ears
much as a hare communicates with air, scent, himself
it is the coming of a season but not a calendar thing
and not a routine at all to me; or, I think, to him:
his territory all over this marginal-hill-country
those days the day comes, and goes those distant
copper-sheathed Scotch trees in the dawn, red of sunset
seem most-visited by dog-marten, and by me –
of course, an illusion. But both of us remember each
and even the hiss of the pines in the wind the first time we met
me stumbling towards a song : he, into dance
so naturally that I marvelled at his slow (going) away
feathering dew rain off bracken a reluctance: I believed
as my reluctance, at the increase in our acquaintance.
Mobile ears sharpening and softening, face black-eyed
black beads of eyes I'd used in taxidermy but
those were glass and these liquid though   hard
elder or bramble but bilberry wideapart eyes!

(from Tea at 40)

snake swirl atter   snake swirl atter

rattler-swirl   every

word tatters

matters man it's like landin mackeral   nothin like it   nothin like in it

spring's mell   wet acid on thin soil is   up   up

out of Wythburndale and Whelpside and Steel End and Dunmail Raise

on the wind   Striding Edge   voice   Swirrel Edge squirrel

squirl   eyesteady while chewing   upcrust edges eye-streaming

Helvellyn   triangulates   from the top you can see catsquirrel

accents   celts   Scots Irish   Manx/ Welsh pass-in

the whole man on   upside-down up the downside of the tree bole

catsquirrel or tree creeper bein looked for   an' waiting to be read

fall now down one side   now down the other   bothways

on Swirrel Edge the rocks face double my testing arrête is double hollow ground

1957, 1971

Vigil trapline

feeling the edges of the mind being crimped
turned in as of a pie crust
pulled at by something in the apart-ness

same-mind, only later asks to be whole
shakes itself as of an insanity
the limbs showed the way out, from cramped

I don't mean the sense of someone
else going beside you, or parallel
yards or even miles away, still
when you are still and not a shadow
anywhere, or a mirage in the glare

Nov 8, 1970
(Scarth Wood)

lights over hills mutually make animate
Cleve-land   cleaved-land
colours that from the thin sill emanate
       deny the sand
myriad stained-glass depths and shines of silica
This has been the longest set of color before the fall
I've ever known in Cleveland, and the latest,
lightest frosts to bring form and color out at once
even though the wind wanted to expose form
the frost did not co-operate to take off leaves
that now hang gold through black and
silver through purple

some still green.

          No sign of marten this day this way

    The marten watched the rain
    spattered the grey Borrowdale
    volcanic rock   in its
    random manner like a marten running, as low,
    on dead bracken as catice

    those highlighting   a quartz
                 inclusion

American Marten, Replacing
The Pine Marten in England

(at the gamekeeper's vermin line)

The ending of leaf-year.
>> Squirrel-cats, as red as Indian, as dead
>> a hundred years after we cleared them off our land
> a panic of birds brought them back.
Slipping from fur farms, trapped origins in America,
>>> to live feral in orthumberland.
> break silhourettes, slim Sitka spruce
> mark mathematical moods of forest
> penetrative of pile Lodgepole pine
> print marten visiting-cards, violet-scats.
>> Inquisitive of woodmen and willed walkers.
Scents in stir.

At White Craig Picnic Site, evening June 4, 1997

then very dark marten
skirting the shadow–shelter
starting my heart!......:steady.
not, as you might expect,
nosing toward the litter

too dark here, already
for this old Compur shutter
she's clear of the clearing,
not leaving it cleaner.
muttering robin and wren
and this reporting pen
temporary witness; gone
in minutes, or seconds
but I may have been given

half an hour to discover
and not disturn her young
beyond starting at their
darkening slready to maturity...

Marten and Wild Cat

For you and me are Holy Grails
these two of the clubtails
swing them in complacency.
Northwards facing we came
yearning for where these other two
burning brambled bracken brake.

Norway this had also happened
Norway where Scotland had been
two in one as we had seemed
twitching time, but patiently
two and two make one, or three…
Norway made cogg cats of trapped
proving that they could be tamed.
But wildcat spaces we never traced
were never ours, though we embrace
marten places at home in them
where marten never bruised a stem
but went away, and came again.

with ACCV, Scotland 1976
revised 2000

(Carcajou)
Marten poems

Their fifty-pounds are compound-interest of ferocity
they told me, the one in the p.v.c., the one in the fur coat
carcajou can kill snowbound elk and even moose
and caribou, getting at belly or especially of course the neck.
So also can the mart attack even sheep deep in the snow
as I now know from Northumberland instances/corpses. And one, at melt
showed a puzzle kill otherwise perplexing. Felt their strength
playing with kits kinetic – catching as they come out
between juggling hot potatoes trot tickling trout
out of the den, all one strong length. Yet after a time or two
lest they become habituated we don't do it.
'Better than barbiturate'   says the one in the (fur) coat
is the jump these wolverines give you: in the heart and at the throat
and for the hairs on the back of a reddened neck or two.

After a month of visits, study, they have only seen my hand
these different weasels alike in being laconic –
but the wolverine more of a haunter of the open land
the barrens, like that other majestic hunter, the falcon
called by Linnaeus rusticolus, country-loving
space-loving, empty-space loving, needing strand
and width of forest and fjord, of mailed-fist gloving,
spruce woods no matter how stunted or spread out
wandering watercourses and muskeg of pools in the summer
ice they both skate on, hardy for their long winter
slide in a swinging motion, confident to some speed
with practice, glissade; when there is no ice or crystal
snow they can do it on shale as I've seen marten go
in Cleveland, Saskatchewan, Alaska, Northern Ontario

In open country, three of my carcajou acquaintances told me, they'd spread
to 20 in 500 sq miles (Wyoming), 40 in 80 sq miles (Montana) and 25 in 700
sq. miles in the Alaska barrens

brushing window his hail
no room on the ledge of it
for arcuate preposterous tail
with this back-ends warm-rain
he's back again, he's back again!
Yet wild squall on that westwind's flail
wiped his backgrease off the windowpane

near as big, he is, as the vixen
he divides hunting birchwood beechwood with
"when fox is scarce, marts is mair" –
so Billy Shields, who lived there before us
but these are too individual to care
about such niceties; both come to us, our
ledge their edge of fear or of the curious.

(1990)

weak as the sound is, it's
squeaking of sucking kits
sits on the slight frost still
deeper than rats behind wainscot
nearer than night stands itself:
a calm on it. No harm to them
of the morning to come, if God will
forester; special apical-meristem
fills new rare life at her tits.

Lines

a loll is the face of mart
a space a map is like, yet neat
condensed energy and edgy senses
wrinkles of ears, ripple of whiskers
all ready bristle function and full

still; I am still, yet missed
too subtle even for his enemy
that change of direction concentration
and just off the head the run to come
and gone

again, from the quick of wind
as also of the living blizzard
found out again by him (I was)
and left for dead, though I had laboured hours to get near

such exercise is toward holiness,
wholeness, just as he talks by the ears
as by the set of the head, inseparable consistence
more than expression of his inquisition
inquisitiveness is not, ever, superficial

for this is a survivor and he listens
'with his heels', his (invisible) sable eyes
which say what we cannot yet quite see
yet are given, if we are able to receive
radio somehow, the gift of self

of 'isness'; which is *his*, not our business
it is self; or all we see of it
breath, footprints, scats, or nothing even
ever misleading. We *know* nothing
which way he went, he went

riddles, still the day sudden
we'll never find out if it was...
or why is all illegible on the edge
of that edginess, expecting everything –
except we windfall, given nothing

Turdus torquatus

talkin at my elbow
as I climbed at his crag
he is not nesting yet
helps me wait-on marten
syllables liquid as the eyes
of marten, of some owls
cascade as a beck rapids
flow seeming smoother than is
its tumble; it has surface sheen
and parallax just as harmony
helped me wait on marten being
at their mating time
and at their cubs' weaning
– in a word, tuning…

Torque is the force in turning
vowels laden with (the) tone
beginning as all do, in breath
shaking this birch and bracken

Marten in juniper thickets
that mistle-thrushes quicken –
juniper is beloved of them

though a North Tyne shepherd
(who loves "misselbirds" well)
hated the juniper, as all "whin"
burned them all out with paraffin

the same left fallen stock for "healthier"
foxes, as his father had, and for marten.

Printed in the United Kingdom
by Lightning Source UK Ltd.
101077UKS00001B/337-378